ANTHOLOGY FOR

Analysis and Performance

For Use in the Theory Classroom

Matthew Bribitzer-Stull
University of Minnesota

New York   Oxford
OXFORD UNIVERSITY PRESS

Oxford University Press is a department of the University of Oxford. It furthers the University's
objective of excellence in research, scholarship, and education by publishing worldwide.

Oxford   New York
Auckland   Cape Town   Dar es Salaam   Hong Kong   Karachi
Kuala Lumpur   Madrid   Melbourne   Mexico City   Nairobi
New Delhi   Shanghai   Taipei   Toronto

With offices in
Argentina   Austria   Brazil   Chile   Czech Republic   France   Greece
Guatemala   Hungary   Italy   Japan   Poland   Portugal   Singapore
South Korea   Switzerland   Thailand   Turkey   UkrainevVietnam

For titles covered by Section 112 of the US Higher Education Opportunity
Act, please visit www.oup.com/us/he for the latest information about
pricing and alternate formats.

Published by Oxford University Press.
198 Madison Avenue, New York, NY 10016
www.oup.com

ISBN 978-0-19-985723-4

Printing number: 9 8 7 6 5 4 3 2 1

Printed in the United States of America on acid-free paper

Contents

Note that a listening list has been established on Naxos Music Library under "Music Anthology for Analysis and Performance" for those instructors and students who have either institutional or personal access to this online resource. Students are encouraged to listen comparatively to multiple recordings of the same works.

Preface for the Instructor

As INSTRUCTORS OF undergraduate music theory, we want our students to understand how music works. To that end many of us teach the same basic material: harmony, counterpoint, voice leading, phrase structure, meter and rhythm, form, score reading, and so forth—all familiar course components, I imagine, to any instructor contemplating using this anthology. Ultimately, all of these various skills and concepts arise from and return in service to the same thing: the music. And therein lies the fundamental problem in teaching music theory nowadays: our students simply don't know the music.

Many students enter our doors having studied their instrument for as many as ten to fifteen years. It is the rare student, though, who knows a wide range of pieces throughout the repertory of tonal art music. Pianists may not have encountered any of the great ensemble pieces for winds; orchestral musicians might know nothing of the rich choral and lieder literature; and singers are often unacquainted with even a single Beethoven string quartet.

Though knowledge of the repertory and its major generic and stylistic trends is an important goal in and of itself—one we hope our colleagues in musicology will be helping us to instill in our students—in theory classes, engaging with it is essential because concepts, from the parallel interrupted period to the Neapolitan, are much easier for students to grasp when heard in context. Moreover, using repertory the students know enables them to immediately connect concept to music on an aural/instinctual level.

There are many serviceable textbooks and anthologies that provide students with the requisite examples from the literature necessary to illustrate concepts studied in class. Unfortunately, most of these examples go unheard. There are a variety of reasons for this sad state of affairs. Musical excerpts in textbooks, for example, are largely ignored by students. Those who read the textbook (all too few in my experience) rarely possess the skill to play the examples at the keyboard or another instrument, or the money to purchase recordings of the examples, or the time to bother going about creating or locating the aural stimulus. Even recorded examples played in class all too easily go in one ear and out the other. Why? Because for many students the points we're illustrating with these bits of music (not to mention the bits themselves) seem irrelevant.

The vast majority of students in an undergraduate theory course care first and foremost about performance or teaching. Thus, it becomes incumbent upon us, the theory instructors, to connect what we want them to learn with those activities they are most motivated to pursue.[1] In my experience, these connections are forged most easily by live performance and use of music the students already know and value.

---

[1]See Marvin (1994), who echoes this sentiment. Although the movement known as Comprehensive Musicianship is all but dead, many of its strengths can be cultivated by individual instructors—in the classroom, the studio, or the rehearsal hall—who wish to link together the various facets of musical training.

The purpose of this anthology is to help instructors make the workings of tonal Western art music from the medieval period to the present day relevant to undergraduates. For that reason, this collection broadens the standard anthology assortment of piano pieces, string quartets, and lieder to include repertory for all the instruments typically studied by music majors.[2] Moreover, the pieces selected are ones many undergraduates will already know from work in private lessons or ensembles. Some of these lie outside what most would consider the established canon of masterworks, but two merits of these peripheral repertories come to mind: they engage the rich bodies of works often known only to players of the instruments for which they were written, and they may provide negative examples (many of us in selecting music for analysis forget that bad music provides different opportunities for learning and growth than does good). The vast majority of the works included in this anthology require only the performing forces and technical abilities present among students in freshman and sophomore theory courses, meaning they can be performed live in class.

Analysis and Performance in the Undergraduate Theory Classroom

These prefatory comments suggest that relationships between performance and analysis cultivated in undergraduate theory classes can reap a rich pedagogical harvest. This has been my personal experience over fifteen years of university-level theory teaching. Since my days as a graduate student, I have endeavored to make live performance a part of the theory classroom, connecting analytic concepts to interpretive decisions in performance (a topic relevant to would-be conductors and teachers, too).[3] What I lacked was a reservoir of pieces for students to play. My most frequent solutions were to ask students to perform examples out of their theory textbooks or to set aside analysis-and-performance days when students would bring in repertory they were working on.

The present collection grows out of both the pieces I collected over the years from these analysis-and-performance sessions and the advice given to me by many colleagues in performance. The pieces are, for the most part, intended to be played live in class (in reduction if necessary, as with some of the concerti movements) so that the instructor can illustrate skills and concepts with live music and, when appropriate, in the context of a discussion with the class and the performer(s) about interpretive decision making. For that reason, I have decided not to

---

[2]Unfortunately, this repertory bias toward keyboard music also permeates the analysis-and-performance literature. Thus, students and instructors looking for published articles dealing with wind literature, for example, are exhorted to write their own.

[3]Analysis and performance has a long tradition in the scholarly and pedagogical literature. Heinrich Schenker's analytic approach, for instance, was strongly geared toward making performance decisions. More recently, Cone (1968) and Berry (1989) have served to jump-start a burgeoning interest in analysis and performance among music theorists. The last two decades bear witness to scores of articles on hypermeter, form, texture, motive, and tonal structure as they relate to performance in both tonal and post-tonal repertories. Of these, most frame their arguments in service of a rapprochement between analysis and performance, implying a gulf between them both in thought and in practice. Those interested in exploring this field of study in greater detail may be interested in consulting the bibliography at the end of this anthology. I also recommend reading Lowe (2003), a wide-ranging article that both broadens and problematizes the relationships between analysis and performance by adding a third variable (interpretation) to the equation, and by drawing in a number of related disciplines (cognitive and information theory primary among them). Finally, Nolan 1993 and Rink 1995 are good general resources for work in analysis and performance.

include specific performance suggestions in the prose introducing each piece; such details are, I think, better left to the taste and judgment of individual teachers and performers.

Over the years, I have also found the following techniques helpful in forging connections between undergraduate music majors and the material taught in the core theory curriculum.[4]

- Focus in-class performance-and-analysis sessions on formal issues. Form, from phrases (including phrase rhythm) and cadences to large formal shapes and salient events, is usually the easiest access point for both performers and listeners into a piece of music. Discussions of harmony, counterpoint, motive, and so forth can then be introduced in this context.
- Communicate regularly with large-ensemble conductors to find out what pieces students will be playing in ensemble during a given a semester. Use excerpts from these pieces to illustrate points in class whenever possible.
- Invite performance faculty into the theory classroom for guest lectures. Many compelling examples of how music theory skills and concepts apply to teaching, performing, and conducting can come from these sessions, especially if the faculty in question include as part of their lectures a performance, a short private lesson, or a coaching session.
- Encourage students to read good analysis. The examples included in Stein (2004) are particularly germane to undergraduate-level study.
- Customize the collection of pieces in this anthology by adding works that faculty at your institution tend to use with first- and second-year students. Include not only solo repertory but also chamber and large-ensemble pieces.
- Take students to area performances by professional musicians. Spend time in class beforehand, giving a pre-concert lecture that focuses on analytic issues.
- Give assignments that stress the practical uses theory and ear-training skills offer (e.g., transcribing cadenzas, arranging pieces for a given ensemble, asking students to go on a "scavenger hunt" for a specific compositional technique within the repertory for their instrument, and so forth).
- Compare arrangements of works to original scores. What principles studied in class seem to guide transcription or arrangement decisions? (Note that, whenever possible, commonly performed arrangements of pieces included in this anthology are called out in the prefatory text for each piece.)
- Compare performance decisions made in different recordings (or live performances) of the same piece. Discuss the analytic implications.[5] Also, compare decisions made in different analyses of the same piece and discuss the performance implications.
- Ask students to keep journals of analytic observations made during practice sessions, ensemble rehearsals, and private lessons. What effects do these have on their process of learning a piece of music?

N.B. All but a few scores in this anthology have been reset. Those few reprinted in their original format were left as such because essential components of the scores' intricacy, poetry, and/or ethos would be lost in transcription.

---

[4]Some of these suggestions are listed and explained further in Folio (1991), 134; Vaughan (2002); and Bribitzer-Stull (2003), 31–32.

[5]This is a reversal of the more usual approach to analysis and performance in which analysis is used to affect performance decisions—an approach adopted in Berry (1989) and one that has been roundly criticized as detrimentally one-sided. For an alternative based on listening to recorded performances, see Leech-Wilkinson (2012).

Preface for the Student

IF YOU HAVE purchased this book, I assume it is because you are studying music at a college or pre-professional level. One of the greatest gifts you can give yourself as a performer, teacher, writer, conductor, or consumer of music is to learn as much repertory as possible. The more music you know, the better you will be able to understand how it works.

To that end, I have compiled the following pieces for you to explore over the course of your music study. I hope you will find that you already know at least one of them, and that there are some that are representative of the repertory for your instrument. Others, I expect, will be foreign to you now but may grow to be old favorites of yours in the years ahead.

I urge you not only to listen to the works contained in this anthology but to use your knowledge of these pieces in two ways: first, to connect your technical study of musical materials to the performance, teaching, conducting, and active listening skills you will be developing simultaneously; and second, to be inspired to seek out other pieces on your own. (If you find you like, for example, the movement from the Mozart Serenade for Winds in C minor, K. 388, you'll be glad to know that there are three more movements in this piece, more than twenty Mozart chamber pieces featuring wind instruments, and many other works for similar ensembles by composers such as Beethoven, Dvořák, and Holst.)

A few years ago, one of my colleagues lamented getting to know the only piece of Brahms's chamber music he had not yet heard. Learning new music is a lifelong pursuit; getting to the end of a body of repertory you have grown to love is often a bittersweet experience, a farewell of sorts. For many of you, that day may be a long way off. Regardless, I envy you the journey of discovery that lies before you; enjoy it every step of the way.

Acknowledgments

THIS ANTHOLOGY'S CONTENTS emerged largely from the advice and expertise of many experienced musicians. I wish to thank the following colleagues for their assistance in helping me select, and in some cases track down, the music in this collection: Lydia Artymiw (University of Minnesota), David Baldwin (University of Minnesota), Mark Bjork (University of Minnesota), J. Lawrie Bloom (Northwestern University), James David Christie (Oberlin Conservatory of Music), Immanuel Davis (University of Minnesota), Michel Debost (Oberlin Conservatory of Music), Daryl Durran (Penn State University), Diana Gannett (University of Michigan), Erin Hannigan (Southern Methodist University), Joan Elaine Holland (University of Michigan), Kristin Wolfe Jensen (University of Texas-Austin), Jeff Keesecker (Florida State University), Korey Konkol (University of Minnesota), Carl Lenthe (Indiana University), Marilyn Mason (University of Michigan), Glenda Maurice (University of Minnesota), Marilyn McDonald (Oberlin Conservatory of Music), John Miller (University of Minnesota), Alan Montgomery (Oberlin Conservatory of Music), Sally O'Reilly (University of Minnesota), Tanya Remenikova (University of Minnesota), Eugene Rousseau (University of Minnesota), Lisa Golas Scoggin (unaffiliated), Peter Slowik (Oberlin Conservatory of Music), and John Tafoya (Indiana University).

Much of this collection evolved from my own classroom analysis-and-performance sessions over the past fifteen years. Works for these sessions were often selected by students who wanted to bring repertory they were rehearsing into music-theory class. To my students past and present at the Eastman School of Music, Penn State University School of Music, and the University of Minnesota School of Music: thank you for introducing me to so many wonderful pieces and for reacquainting me with so many others.

Among my performance colleagues at the University of Minnesota, five—Lydia Artymiw, Tom Ashworth, Mark Bjork, John deHann, and Jean del Santo—have consented thus far to join my classes to discuss the role analysis can play in teaching, in rehearsing, and in interpretive decision making. I hope that this anthology can repay in some small way the spirit of collaboration you all brought to my own teaching.

I also owe an enormous debt of gratitude to the three University of Minnesota music theory graduate students who assisted me with indexing. They are Mark Arneson, Jessica Narum, and Jeremy Orosz. Their work was made possible by a generous grant from the University of Minnesota's Imagine Fund. This same fund and a Society for Music Theory Subvention Grant also subsidized the Herculean task of engraving the scores afresh—a task accomplished with alacrity and professionalism by Colin Holter, another graduate student at the University of Minnesota. Three other students of mine provided assistance with selecting and locating music and my thanks go also to them: Andrew Brobston, Markus Hahn, and Karen Jennings.

Of course, this anthology would never have come to be without the interest and enthusiasm of Jan Beatty at Oxford University Press, who gave me invaluable advice in the project's early stages. Richard Carlin, Nicole Lefebvre, Sheena Kowalski, and Katherine Albis picked up for Jan when she departed Oxford, and shepherded the book to its completion. Pamela Hanley, Thomas Finnegan, and the layout team at Oxford greatly added to the quality of the finished product with their attention to detail in both the prose and the musical examples. Repertory suggestions and ideas for additional material provided by the anonymous reviews was likewise of great value. My heartfelt thanks go to them as well.

As is customary, my final acknowledgement goes to my husband of seventeen years, Jason, who tolerated both my excitement—as I played sections of the works in this anthology for him—and my frustration as I grumbled over the seemingly endless process of indexing. Although I know this anthology is of little use to you in the actuarial profession, I hope you see its completion as a tangible marker of the love and support you have shown me over the years, and of the life—filled with music—that we have shared together.

It goes without saying that any errors or inconsistencies that remain are my responsibility alone.

1. Hymn: *Ut queant laxis*

ANONYMOUS

(medieval)

❖

Musicologists attribute the origins of solfège to Guido of Arezzo's use of this tune. Look at the beginning of each line of text in the chant below. The opening syllable and attendant pitch should form a familiar pattern when considered sequentially.

So that your servants may,
with loosened voices,
resound the wonders of your deeds,
clean the guilt from our stained lips,
O Saint John.

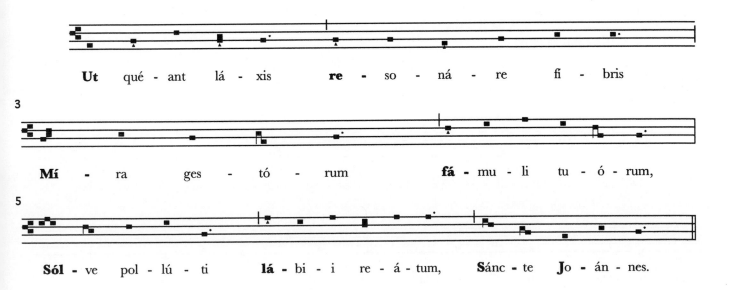

Ut qué - ant lá - xis **re** - so - ná - re fí - bris

3

Mí - ra ges - tó - rum **fá** - mu - li tu - ó - rum,

5

Sól - ve pol - lú - ti **lá** - bi - i re - á - tum, **Sánc** - te **Jo** - án - nes.

2. Sequence: *Dies Irae*

ANONYMOUS
(13th century)
❖

The word *sequence* can mean many things in musical parlance. One meaning refers to a type of chant repertory with a long and intricate history. A synoptic definition would be as follows: the sequence is a lengthy, sacred Latin text set syllabically. In the sixteenth century, the Council of Trent (1543–63) eliminated all but seven sequences from the liturgy. Of those that remain, the *Dies Irae* and *Stabat Mater* are the most important in the history of music, with literally hundreds of settings of each. Almost from its inception, the sequence was deemed appropriate for polyphonic music in which the original tune was set among other vocal lines, a practice that has continued to the current day. The *Dies Irae* appears in both popular and art-music repertories to evoke the solemnity and dread of the Day of Judgment.

The day of wrath, that day
Will dissolve the world in ashes
As foretold by David and the sibyl!
(first stanza only)

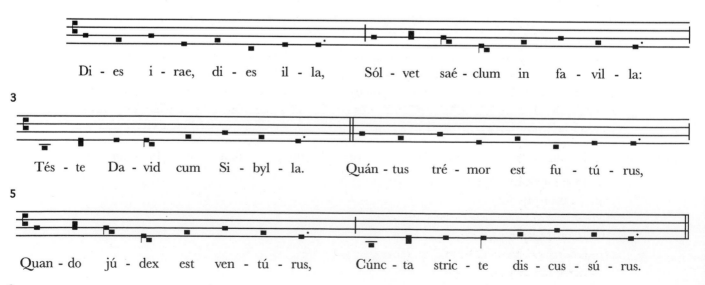

Di - es   i - rae, di - es   il - la,   Sól - vet   saé - clum   in   fa - vil - la:

Tés - te   Da - vid   cum   Si - byl - la.   Quán - tus   tré - mor   est   fu - tú - rus,

Quan - do   jú - dex   est   ven - tú - rus,   Cúnc - ta   stric - te   dis - cus - sú - rus.

3. Aucun ont trouvé— Lonc tans (late 13th century)

PIERRE DE LA CROIX

(mid-13th century–early 14th century)

❖

Pierre de la Croix (also known as Petrus de Cruce) played an important role in the history of Western music notation. In short, he introduced note values in which basic beats (breves) could be broken up into a variety of subdivisions—up to seven—called semibreves. He used these faster note values to create a spoken-text rhythm called *parlando* that contrasted with more sustained sections of long-note singing.

The work here is an isorhythmic motet from the late thirteenth century. The motet genre emerged from earlier Notre Dame organum, specifically its faster-moving clausula sections, and typically comprised three parts. These parts were most usually arranged as follows: the lowest voice—called the *tenor*—sang long, sustained tones drawn from a short melismatic section of existing plainchant, which was organized into a rhythmic pattern repeated throughout the motet. Above the tenor were two newly composed parts—the *duplum* (or motetus) and *triplum*—that were textually and harmonically independent from the tenor; they sang different texts (which could be related to the tenor in topic or not, and could even be in a language other than the tenor) and often featured grating dissonances with the tenor. Note that this score is a transcription of an older form of notation. The notes with slashes through their stems are meant to indicate that performance of the original would have most likely involved less precise rhythmic values at these spots than the note values in the modern notation.

The motet originally developed within the church but quickly devolved into a popular secular genre even when liturgical plainsong tenors were used. This is the case with *Aucun ont trouvé—Lonc tans*. The title indicates the opening texts of the *duplum* and *triplum* voices, in this case both French courtly love texts. That these two texts are performed simultaneously gives this work an ironic combination of jaded and ingenuous views on unrequited love.

TRIPLUM
There are men who live by writing songs,
but I am inspired
by a love that so fills my heart with joy
that I can't stop myself writing a song.
For a faire and lovely lady, of high repute,
has made me love her

and I, who have pledged myself to serve her
all my days, loyally
and with no thought of betrayal,
shall sing, for from her do I hold such a sweet bequest
that it alone can give me joy.
It is this thought which soothes my sweet sorrow
and gives me hope of a cure for it.
At the same time,
Love may well complain of my arrogance
and hold me prisoner all my days;
I wouldn't think the worse of her for that.
She knows how to lay siege so cleverly
that there is no defense against her;
neither might nor rank
is of the slightest use.
And if it pleases her to give back my ransom at her will,
I shall be her captive and give my heart as surety
by putting it completely at her disposal.
And I beg for mercy, since I have no alternative,
no other words to say for myself.

DUPLUM
Long have I refrained from singing,
but now I have reason to show my joy
since true love has led me to desire
the most accomplished lady
to be found in the whole world.
No other can be compared to her,
and when I so love such a precious lady
that I have great pleasure merely in thinking about her,
well do I know
that a life of true love
is very pleasant,
whatever people say.

TENOR
ANNUN(TIANTES) from the Gradual
Omnes de Saba for Epiphany.

Translation: Michael J. Freeman

4. Saltarello

ANONYMOUS
(14th century)
❖

This work is an instrumental dance from fifteenth-century Tuscany called a *saltarello*, a word that was used for a variety of Italian dance forms but that, at this time, connoted jumping or leaping. (Listen for frequent leaping intervals in the melody.) It opens with a short, repeated section (A) that concludes with one of two endings, tonally open for the first repetition, and tonally closed for the second, a structure characteristic of medieval dance music. Two more melodic ideas (B and C) appear later and alternate with the opening (A) music to form an arrangement we can summarize as ABACACA.

Prima pars.

1. **2.**

Prima pars is repeated

Secunda pars.

Tertia pars.

Quarta pars.

Tertia pars is repeated

5. Trotto

ANONYMOUS

(14th century)

❖

The *trotto* is another textless, monophonic dance that, like the saltarello, survives in a fifteenth-century Tuscan manuscript. The one here, like the saltarello, features three distinct melodic sections. As expected, the A section has two endings, one open and one closed. It is followed by a repeated B section, which is then elaborated before introducing a short C fragment (lengthened in later iterations) that returns as an interjection between subsequent A statements.

6. Se je souspir
(mid–14th century)

GUILLAUME DE MACHAUT
(1300–77)

Machaut's settings of courtly love texts are more concerned with musical form (melodic and rhythmic figures repeated throughout a piece) than those of such earlier poets as Wolfram von Eschenbach, who used a declaimed song-speech approach. As such, Machaut's works are referred to as *chansons*, or "songs," rather than just poems. Chansons in the earlier fourteenth century were typically performed by one voice, so when Machaut began developing polyphonic chansons for multiple voices—to poetry he had written himself, no less!—Europe took note.

This chanson is in the form of a virelai, one of three *formes fixes* ("fixed forms") popular in late Medieval France. (The others were the ballade and the rondeau.) The virelai features repeated chunks of melodic material organized into a four-part ABBA form. Listen to how the A section ("If I sigh…" ("Se je souspir") to "dear lady" ("Dame, ne voy.")) returns at "that I willingly…" ("Qu'a vous tres"). Between these two iterations of A material, the B section is sounded twice; once at "Your sweet demeanor…" ("Vostre dous main-tieng") and again at "… and your guileless candor…" ("Et vo maniere sans effroy,"). After this initial presentation, the A and B material both return later.

If I sigh deeply
and affectionately,
sobbing quietly,
it is, by my faith,
for you, upon whose loveliness
I feast, dear lady.

Your sweet demeanor, simple and coy,
your elegant attire,
careful and pleasing,
and your guileless candor
have captivated me
so smoothly
that I willingly
make you

a loving gift
of this heart of mine,
which far from you
knows neither joy nor pleasure.

If I sigh, *etc.*

Thus the great suffering I bear
in secret is more than any
I have heard of.
But, by my soul,
I accept it
very humbly.
By easing my burden
a little,
with one single deed,
you might make my life
as happy as a king's,
so I believe.

If I sigh, *etc.*

Translation: David Munrow

Se   je sous-pir par-fon-de-ment   Et___ ten-dre-ment Pleure en re-coy, C'est par ma foy, Pour
Qu'à vous tres a-mou-reu-se-ment   En-tie-re-ment Doing et ot-troy Le cuer de moy Qui

vous, quant vo fai-tis corps gent, Da-me,__ ne-voy.   Vos-tre dous main-tieng sim-ple et coy, Vo bel__ ar-roy, Cointe
loing de vous es-ba-te-ment N'a n'es-ba-noy.   Et vo ma-nie-re sans__ ef-froy, Pris m'ont__ cil__ troy Si

1.
et__ plai - sant

2.
dou - ce - ment

7. Ave maris stella
(mid–15th century)

JOHN DUNSTABLE
(c. 1390–1453)
❖

John Dunstable's work is exemplary of the *contenance angloise*, or English style, a type of writing in the first half of the fifteenth century that stressed the sweet sounds of thirds and sixths as consonances (whereas at this time on the continent these intervals still functioned as dissonances, striving for resolution). Dunstable's style of text setting was also remarkable for its clarity; often, most or all of the voices sing the same syllables at the same time, aiding comprehension. This homorhythmic character was not necessarily representative of polyphonic music in general.

Both the use of thirds and the clear declamation of text can be heard in Dunstable's only surviving hymn setting, *Ave maris stella*. Listen to how this work alternates plainsong (monody) with counterpoint (polyphony), stanza by stanza. Listen also to the three-voice cadences. Some are the so-called double-leading-tone variety—a hallmark of medieval composition—in which $\sharp\hat{4}$ and $\hat{7}$ both rise by half step (to $\hat{5}$ and $\hat{1}$, respectively) while the lowest voice sings $\hat{2}$ moving down by whole step to $\hat{1}$.

> Hail, star of the sea,
> bountiful mother of God
> and ever Virgin,
> happy gate of heaven.
> Taking that Ave
> from the mouth of Gabriel,
> preserve us in peace,
> giving Eve a new name.
>
> Loose the chains of the bound,
> bring light to the blind,
> drive out our ills,
> invoke all things good.

Show thyself to be a mother,
may he who was born for us
receive our prayers
through thee.

Singular virgin,
more gentle than all,
absolve us from sin and
make us gentle and pure.

Grant us a pure life,
prepare a safe way,
that in seeing Jesus
we may rejoice for ever.

8. *Nuper rosarum flores* (1436)

GUILLAUME DUFAY
(1397–1474)
❖

Dufay composed *Nuper rosarum flores* for the March 25, 1436 consecration of the Florence cathedral. The name of the cathedral—Santa Maria del Fiore (St. Mary of the Flower)—was the inspiration for the title, and the opening lines of text refer to Pope Eugene IV's gift of a golden rose for the high altar. Dufay's isorhythmic motet is unusual in a number of regards, not least among them being the use of two tenor lines, canonic in pitch (*color*) and with an interlocking repeated rhythm (*talea*). The motet divides into four sections, contradicting the poetic structure of the text in the upper voices. Scholars continue to argue whether or not the proportions of Dufay's musical structure mimic the proportions of Brunelleschi's dome for the cathedral.

UPPER VOICES
Recently garlands of roses
were given by the Pope—
despite a terrible winter—
to you, heavenly Virgin,
dedicated in a pious and holy fashion,
a temple of great ingenuity,
to be a perpetual adornment.
Today the vicar
of Jesus Christ and of Peter
a successor, Eugenius,
has to this vast
temple with his hands
and holy liquors
deigned to consecrate.

Therefore, sweet parent
of your son, and daughter,
virgin of virgins
to you the Florentines
devoted as a people,
together in mind and body
on earth, pray to you.

By your prayer
to the crucified and worthy,
your second flesh,
their Lord,
grant us benefit
and receive pardons
for their transgression.
Amen.

TENORS
Magnificent is this place

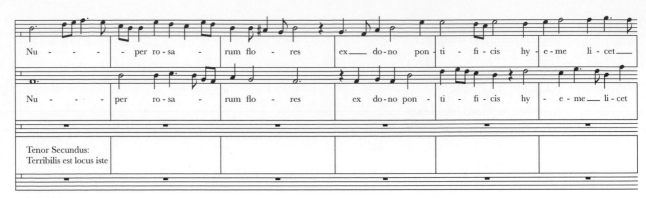

Nu - - - per ro - sa - rum flo - res ex do - no pon - ti - fi - cis hy - e - me li - cet

Nu - - - per ro - sa - rum flo - res ex do - no pon - ti - fi - cis hy - e - me li - cet

Tenor Secundus:
Terribilis est locus iste

Tenor Primus:
Terribilis est locus iste

hor - ri - da ti - - - - - - bi, vir - go ce-li - ca, pi - e et - sanc-

hor - ri - da ti - - - - - - - bi, vir - go ce - li - ca, pi - e et -

- te de - - di - tum gran-dis tem - plum ma - chi - ne con-de-co-

sanc - te de - di - tum gran - dis templum ma - chi - ne con-

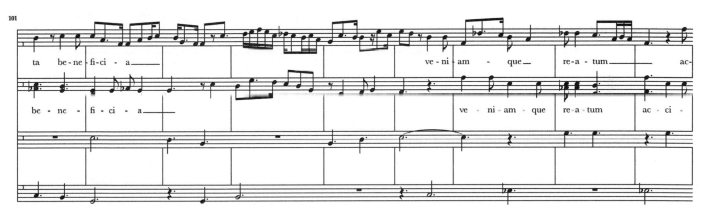

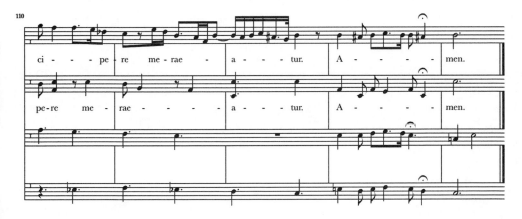

9. Je ne vis oncques la pareille
(mid–15th century)

GILLES BINCHOIS
(c. 1400–60)

Compare this chanson to the one preceding by Machaut. Both are *formes fixes*, though the Binchois piece features a different organization of melodic material, known as rondeau. Specifically, the italicized refrain in the translation below returns each time with the same music. Can you hear it? Compare this song also to John Dunstaple's *Ave maris stella*. Both composers set lines of text to musical phrases that end in cadences. But, even though many of Dunstaple's are the double-leading tone cadence, Binchois was fond of the "under-third" cadence, in which the leading tone, or $\hat{7}$ of the scale, does not ascend directly to tonic ($\hat{1}$), as we are used to in later tonal music, but rather first descends to $\hat{6}$ and from there up a third to $\hat{1}$. Thus the final cadential gesture features the third below the tonic, or the "under third."

I have never seen the equal
of you, my gracious lady,
for your beauty, upon my soul,
is unequalled by any others.
When I see you, I marvel
and ask, Is this Our Lady?

I have never seen the equal
of you, my gracious lady.
Your very great sweetness awakes
my spirit, and my eye opens up
my heart, which I may say boldly,
for I am prepared to serve you.

I have never seen the equal. . . .

Je___ ne vis onc - ques la pa - reil - - le De vous___ ma gra - ci - eu - se___

___ da - me. Car vo___ be - aul - té___ est sur___ mon___ a - me,

Sur___ tou - tes___ aul - tres non pa - reil - le.___

10. Kyrie from *Missa Prolationum* (mid–15th century)

JOHANNES OCKEGHEM
(c. 1410–97)

One of the main technical developments in composition that separated the Renaissance from the earlier Medieval period was the emergence of counterpoint, a method of writing two or more interdependent musical lines in which vertical considerations of consonance and dissonance are just as important as horizontal considerations of good melodic writing. Some contrapuntal pieces feature a pre-extant melody, or *cantus firmus*; others work with imitative techniques, as in this work by Johannes Ockeghem.

Among the early contrapuntalists, Ockeghem is perhaps the greatest. He was one of the first to dispense with the cantus firmus in favor of imitative counterpoint. More importantly, he was able to write difficult counterpoint such that the end result never sounded forced, but rather exemplified the Renaissance taste for clarity and simple beauty. This mass movement is one such example. It features two pairs of voices; in each pair, one line is performed against itself, but at a different speed, a type of canon known as *prolation* or *mensuration* canon.

The Kyrie is the first movement of the mass and the only mass text in Greek (rather than Latin). Given the tripartite text (see below), composers often relied on a three-part structure; Ockeghem is no exception. Note that each line of the text comprises a musical section that features a canon at a different interval.

Kyrie eleison.	Lord have mercy on us.	Canon at the unison
Christe eleison.	Christ have mercy on us.	Canon at the second
Kyrie eleison.	Lord have mercy on us.	Canon at the third

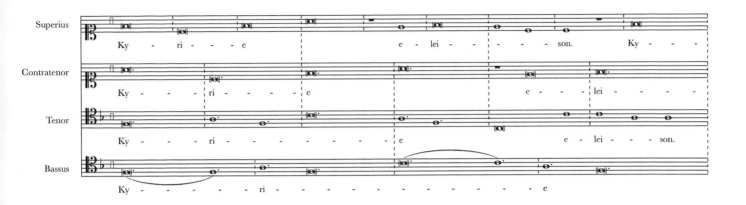

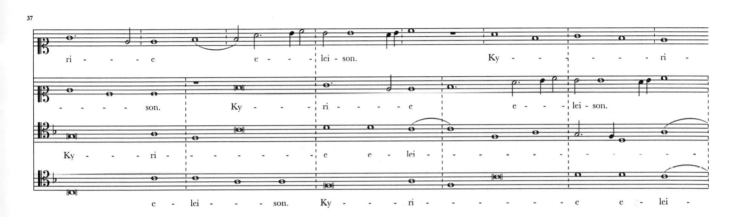

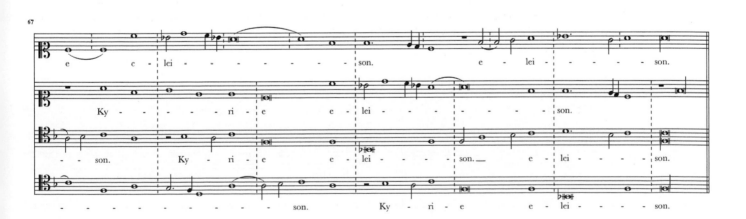

Pausans ascendit per unum tonum

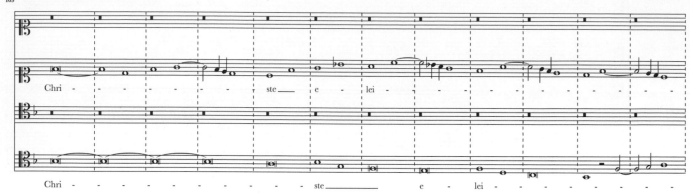

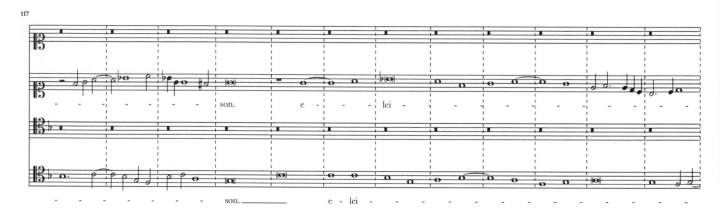

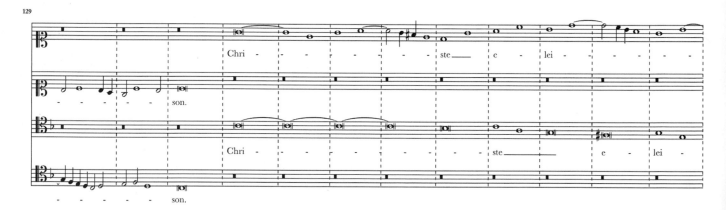

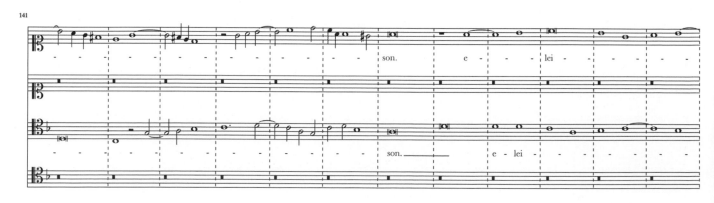

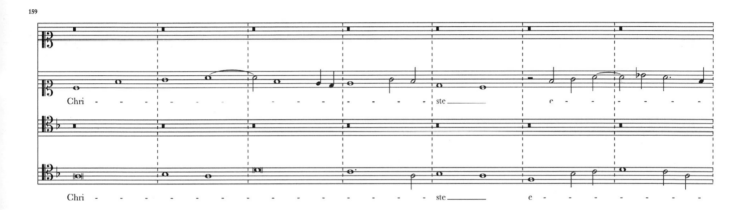

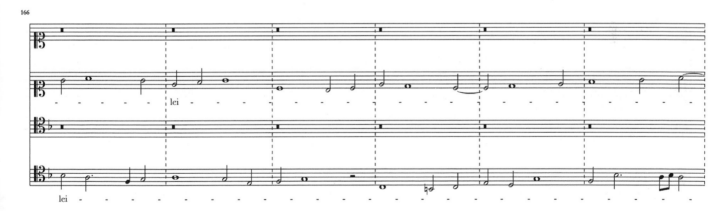

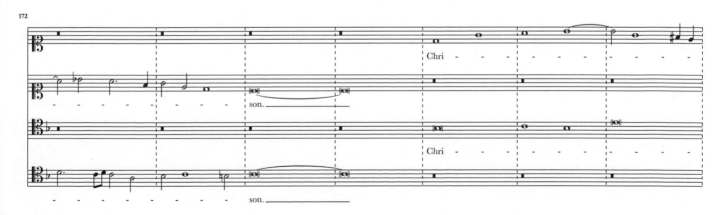

179

186

192

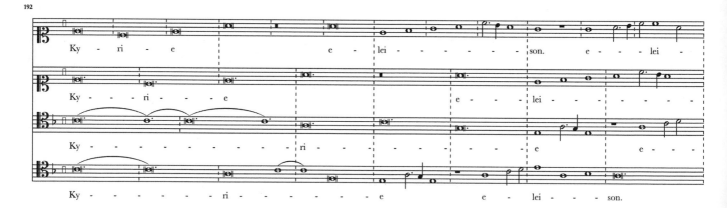

240

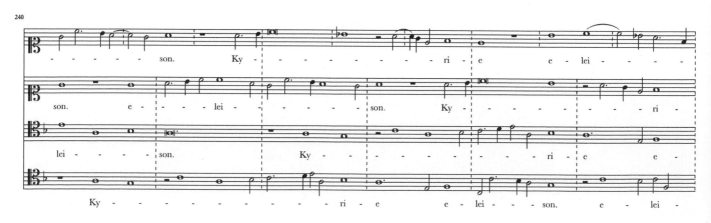

276

11. Kyrie from *Missa La sol fa re mi* (early 16th century)

JOSQUIN DES PREZ
(c. 1450/55–1521)

❖

You will no doubt notice differences between this Kyrie and the one by Ockeghem. Among the most striking is Josquin's use of a repeated motive, one that contemporary musicians might have assigned the hexachordal solfège syllables la, sol, fa, re, mi (that is the sixth, fifth, fourth, second, and third notes of a six-note, diatonic collection). This practice was not uncommon in the Renaissance period and was often referred to as *soggetto cavato* (carved subject). The subjects often pay homage to patrons of music or reference textual mottos. Here, "La sol fa re mi" is intended to mimic the sound of the Italian phrase, "Lascia fare mi" (leave me alone). Pay special attention to how Josquin works the subject into the musical fabric throughout, and how he transforms it.

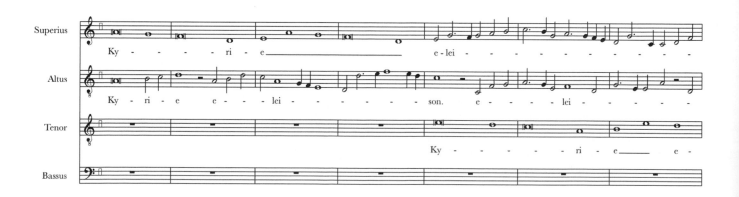

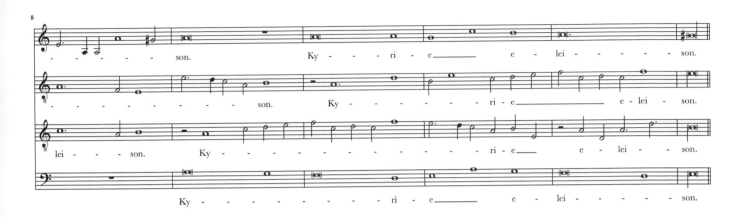

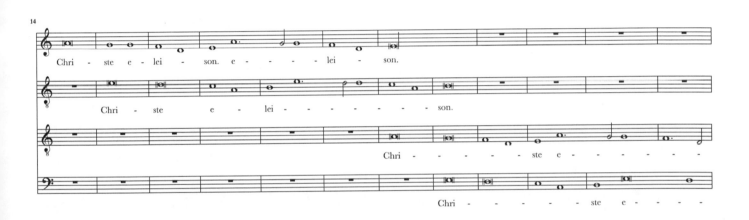

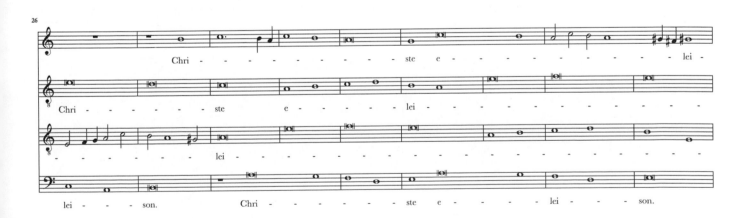

12. La Mourisque
(1551)

TIELMAN SUSATO
(1510/15–1570?)

❖

Included in Tielman Susato's collection of published dance music is an example of the Moresco (or Morris dance as it is called in English). The Moresco was one of many courtly dances in the fifteenth century, but it was not confined to the nobility alone; paid professionals performed it as popular entertainment, and wealthy artisans danced it as a pastime. The dance took a variety of forms, but all of them were inspired by examples brought to Spain by invading Moorish forces. They included sinuously exotic solo dances, mock battle scenes, and competitive miming performed in a circle. Most were done in blackface (to approximate the darker skin of the Moors) and the dancers often wore bells.

It follows that music for the Moresco also took diverse forms since there was no set choreography or meter. Rather, the music was written to complement the often-exaggerated movements of the dancers. The example by Susato features a clear Renaissance texture and regular four-bar groups that can be counted just like the beats in a bar, creating another level of metric regularity musicians call *hypermeter*. As in the Saltarello and Trotto examples, Susato's "La Mourisque" (a French spelling of the dance) features an A section comprising a pair of phrases with two endings. A is repeated and then followed by a contrasting B section, also comprising a repeated pair of phrases. The music as performed would alternate these two sections, closing with a return to the opening material.

13. Fyer, Fyer!
(1595)

THOMAS MORLEY
(1557/58–1602)

By 1600, nearly all English composers had become engrossed in the madrigal. Or, to be more specific, they had become engrossed with the "light" madrigal style of Italian composers such as Marenzio, Ferretti, and Gastoldi (as opposed to the more serious and recondite chromatic practices of composers such as Gesualdo and Lasso). Although the English altogether never wrote as many madrigals as even Marenzio alone, their wholesale adoption of a foreign musical model is striking; rarely in the history of Western music have musicians embraced a foreign influence so quickly and so wholeheartedly.

English madrigalists, as a rule, imitated the more lighthearted style of Italian madrigal, eschewing the more expressionistic and radical compositions that deviated from typical Renaissance compositional practice in order to set highly emotional texts. Nevertheless, we still hear some anguished word painting in Morley's "Fyer, fyer!" Listen, particularly, to the use of suspensions (accented dissonances) on the text "Ay me." This is an English translation of the Italianate madrigal cry of anguish *Ohi me.* We note also in Morley's setting the use of "fa la la" lyrics common to the English madrigal refrain, but absent from the Italian.

Fyer, fyer!
My heart!
O, I burn me!
Alas! Fa la la la la.
O help, alas!
Ay me, I sit and cry me
And call for help,
but none comes nigh me.
Fa la la la la.
I burn, alas!
Ay me, will none come quench me?
O cast water on and drench me!
Fa la la la la.

14. *Asciugate i begli occhi*
(1611)

CARLO GESUALDO
(c. 1561–1613)
❖

Among music students, Carlo Gesualdo's reputation is well known, for certain details of his biography as much as for his adventurous music. Gesualdo's compositions demonstrate proficiency in a variety of genres, both sacred and secular, but it is for his madrigals that he is best known. In them, every verbal image is matched by a separate musical figure. This creates a sectional form, really more of a succession of short musical formulations than an overarching narrative gesture. It also makes for highly expressive music, and Gesualdo was not one to shy away from eccentric compositional practices in bringing a text to life.

Asciugate i begli occhi is representative of Gesualdo's later madrigal style. In it, we hear extreme chromaticism (like other avant-garde musicians of the late sixteenth century, Gesualdo was inspired by the fully chromatic keyboard created by Nicolo Vicentino) and orthodox dissonance treatments that, when combined, create a most strikingly unorthodox composite effect. Finally, the text itself is typical of Gesualdo's predilections. Eschewing pastoral and narrative poetry, he preferred—perhaps not surprisingly, given what we know about his life—to set texts about love, death, and psychological pain.

> Dry those lovely eyes,
> alas, my beloved, do not weep
> if you see me wandering far away from you.
> For, ah, I must weep alone and in misery,
> because as I part from you,
> I suffer such bitter pain that my days are numbered.

15. "A Shoemaker's Wife a Toye," arr. for marimba by Rebecca Kite
(early 17th century)

JOHN DOWLAND
(1563?– 1626)

❖

John Dowland was active as a musician during England's Tudor Dynasty. He is best known for his many lute songs, which were often based on dance forms. How do meter, large-scale repetition, and form in this work—here arranged for marimba but originally a lute song—contribute to the sense of dance music?

16. *Cruda Amarilli*
(1605)

CLAUDIO MONTEVERDI
(1567–1643)

"Cruel Amaryllis" is among the most notorious works in the history of Western music. Its composition and reception marked the end of an era and the dawning of a *seconda pratica* ("second practice") whose tenets still influence compositional decisions today.

On the face of it, "Cruel Amaryllis" is unassuming, just one of many five-part madrigals in a series of works published by the Italian composer Claudio Monteverdi. Its text (see below) is the sarcastic reaction of a spurned lover. To capture the essence of the words, however, Monteverdi did the unthinkable—at least, to those trained in the "prima pratica" style of Renaissance counterpoint espoused by the sixteenth-century theorist Gioseffo Zarlino and exemplified in the sacred works of Palestrina.

Monteverdi's crime was none other than presentation of unprepared and—even worse—unresolved dissonances. Around the turn of the seventeenth century, the conservative theorist Giovanni Maria Artusi, himself a student of Zarlino, attacked such improprieties of "modern" music. Monteverdi and others leapt to the defense of new music, espousing the view of *seconda pratica* composers that the tones should be the mistress of the text; that is, "rules" for composing good music don't necessarily apply when its principal aim is text expression.

> Cruel Amaryllis, who with your name
> to love, alas, bitterly you teach.
> Amaryllis, more than the white privet
> pure, and more beautiful,
> but deafer than the asp,
> and fiercer and more elusive.
> Since telling I offended you,
> I shall die in silence.

17. Largo from Trio Sonata in C Major, Op. 4, No. 1 *(1694)*

ARCANGELO CORELLI
(1653–1713)
❖

The term *trio sonata* often confuses beginning students of Baroque music. Though there are three main *parts* (two melodic lines and a basso continuo), there are four *players* in a trio sonata. In this example the two melodic parts are played by violins. The bass line is notated for violone, a low string instrument, but could also have been played by many other single-line bass instruments (the bassoon and chittarone among them). Moreover, the bass line is duplicated by the left hand of the keyboard. The score here has been *realized* (i.e., written out according to the figures below the staves) in the right hand of the basso continuo, though normally this would not be part of the written score. Rather, the keyboard player would improvise the right-hand part, according to the figures.

PRELUDIO. Largo

18. Largo from Trio Sonata in C Minor, Op. 4, No. 11 (1694)

ARCANGELO CORELLI
(1653–1713)
❖

Like the previous work by Corelli, this score features a realized figured bass. Performers and editors don't, however, always take the composer's figured bass notations as absolute commands; they are often treated more as suggestions. Can you find any points in this work where the realization doesn't seem to match the figures? Do you find the editor's liberties excusable, or even preferable?

19. Sonata for Bassoon (Cello, Trombone) No. 6 in C Major *(1733)*

JOHN ERNEST GALLIARD
(1666/87?– 1747)
❖

Composers writing before the Classic era sometimes didn't specify instruments in their scores. Thus pieces with instrumental lines in the treble clef are often played by violins, flutes, or oboes, and those written in bass and tenor clef are often played by bassoon, cello, or trombone. The music will, however, pose technical challenges that vary with the instruments. Compare three performances of this work by different instrumentalists and how they each solve technical challenges in service to musical challenges.

Sarabanda

Menuet alternat

20. Messe Pour les Convents
(1690)

FRANÇOIS COUPERIN
(1668–1733)

❖

These two movements are part of the *Messe pour les convents*, one of two masses Couperin included in his *Pieces d'orgue*. The *Messe pour les convents* is the more informal of the two, lacking the cantus firmus technique and majestic settings of its counterpart. It may have been used in conjunction with one of the plainchant masses written in France near the end of the seventeenth century.

"PLEIN JEU. PREMIER COUPLET DU KYRIE"

"CHROMHORNE SUR LA TAILLE. 5ᴱ COUPLET"

21. Concerto for Two Oboes and Strings in D Minor, RV 535 (early 18th century)

ANTONIO VIVALDI
(1678–1741)
❖

The music of Antonio Vivaldi is exemplary for its use of *Fortspinnung*—the spinning out of short motivic ideas into sequences, phrases, or even an entire work. In each movement of this concerto, see if you can identify one or more motives whose development (be it transposition, sequence, inversion, rhythmic and intervallic augmentation or diminution, and so forth) comprises large chunks of the movement.

Largo

22. Bassoon Sonata in F Minor
(early to mid–18th century)

GEORG PHILIP TELEMANN
(1681–1767)

❖

Today, we are taught that Johann Sebastian Bach was the greatest composer of the late Baroque period; textbooks even go so far as to align the conventional end of the Baroque era with the date of Bach's death. During the early and middle eighteenth century, though, Bach's reputation was eclipsed by that of his contemporary, Georg Philip Telemann. Telemann stood at the forefront of musical innovation in the late Baroque and helped redefine the role of the professional musician by participating in musical life and education outside his "day job" as Kapellmeister in Hamburg. He was also the most prolific composer of his day, the author of hundreds and hundreds of works for virtually every known instrument, ensemble, and genre. The f-minor bassoon sonata has remained a staple of the repertory for bassoonists as well as a favorite of trombonists, whose dearth of eighteenth-century repertory might excuse them from borrowing from that of other instruments. What does "sonata" mean in the title of this work? Is either movement in sonata form?

Vivace

23. Fantasy for Solo Violin No. 12 in A Minor
(1735), arr. for viola

GEORG PHILIP TELEMANN
(1681–1767)

❖

The central topic in most undergraduate core music theory courses is harmony. But what do we make of harmony when only melody is present? At times the melody is "compound," that is, it arpeggiates through a harmonic progression. At other times, the melody only suggests or implies a harmony, often through evocation of melodic patterns that have common harmonizations. Does an understanding of the implied harmony in this piece lead to better understanding of phrase structure and form? What implications does this have for performance decisions?

24. Fantasy for Solo Flute No. 9 in E Major
(1732–33)

GEORG PHILIP TELEMANN
(1681–1767)
❖

A problem faced by singers and wind players is where to breathe. In textures where cadences and rests are frequent, this isn't a problem. But what about the *moto perpetuo* texture below? Analysis can help determine where implied phrase endings (i.e., cadences) occur, and suggest places for rubato and breathing. Even string and percussion players—though not faced with the imperative of making decisions about breathing—can benefit from considering it, especially if among their aims is emulation of a singing style and tone. Knowledge of the genre—fantasy (also, fantasia)—may be of some assistance in this regard. Fantasy pieces were meant to sound improvisatory and free in execution (and may, in fact, have arisen compositionally from extemporaneous improvisation). Their harmonic structures, metric and phrase groups, melodic content, and form are often looser than one would expect in other eighteenth-century genres, thus permitting a freedom with tempo and phrasing that would allow gaps for breathing. Such interpretive details are, of course, left up to the performer.

Affettuoso

25. Nine Settings of a Chorale Tune: *"O Haupt voll Blut und Wunden" (various)*

JOHANN SEBASTIAN BACH

(1685–1750)

❖

The settings below are drawn from a number of Bach's works. In each, the melody derives from an old tune first published by Hans Leo Hassler in 1601 as a love song entitled "Mein G'müt ist mir verwirret" ("My heart is all excited"). German translations of sacred texts were later set to Hassler's tune by the composer Paul Gerhardt. Among them are texts that Bach used, and that are still known today, such as "Herzlich tut mich verlange" ("I yearn with heartfelt longing"), "O Haupt voll Blut und Wunden" ("O sacred head, now wounded"), and "Befiehl du deine Wege" ("Commit thou all thy griefs").

The four-part chorale texture was among Bach's favored mediums of instruction and also served as the congregational hymn of the German Protestant church service. It is thus unsurprising that Bach commonly used four-part chorale style (*stylus simplex*) for the closing movements of his cantatas and at the end of subsections in the passions and oratorios. Note how the writing suits performance by untrained musicians: it uses an easily singable melody characterized by the "speaking" quality of the part writing and the harmonies, rather than aiming for recondite word-painting figures.

The melody in the examples below is worthy of study. Does it imply a given key or scale? What is it about this melody that enabled Bach to pen diverse harmonic settings of it? And why do so many of them seem tonally open, ambiguous, or unfinished? Begin by analyzing the relatively clear, diatonic settings in 25C, D, and I below. Compare these to the highly chromatic setting in 25F and the tonally ambiguous settings in 25A, B, and G. Though the chorales appear simple, even labeling harmonies with Roman numerals can prove difficult in many cases. Why?

"O HAUPT VOLL BLUT UND WUNDEN," *St. Matthew Passion*, **BWV 244**

"BEFIEHL DU DEINE WEGE," *St. Matthew Passion*

"WENN ICH EINMAL SO SCHEIDEN," *St. Matthew Passion*

"ICH WILL HIER"/"ERKENNE MICH, MEIN HUTER," *St. Matthew Passion*

"WIE SOLL ICH DICH EMPFANGEN," *Christmas Oratorio*, **BWV 248**

"UND OB GLEICH ALLE TEUFEL," *Schau, lieber Gott, wie meine Feind*, **BWV 153**

"DER LEIB ZWAR IN DER ERDEN," *Komm, du süsse Todesstunde*, BWV 161

"BEFIEHL DU DEINE WEGE," CHORALE BWV 270

"BEFIEHL DU DEINE WEGE," CHORALE BWV 271

26. Fantasia and Fugue in G Minor, BWV 542
(ca. 1720–25)

JOHANN SEBASTIAN BACH
(1685–1750)

❖

This work, along with the comparable *Passacaglia and Fugue in C Minor*, exemplifies the massive proportions Bach's organ writing could achieve. The fugue alone modulates to all of g minor's closely related keys and ends with a tour de force tonic recapitulation of double- and triple-invertible counterpoint passages that occurred earlier in the work. Among the many other compositional techniques explored in it, florid melody, chromaticism, and sequences by descending fifths feature prominently. The large-scale key scheme of the fugue is particularly interesting. Can you uncover a pattern?

Fuga

27. Prelude in G Minor (originally for lute in C Minor), BWV 999 (*c. 1720*), *arr. for marimba*

JOHANN SEBASTIAN BACH
(1685–1750)
❖

This work was originally written for the lute, a fretted, plucked string instrument that gradually declined in popularity across the eighteenth century. Notice the opening harmonic gambit, which features a low tonic pitch. Often called "pedal" tones after the use of the organ pedal for these notes, on a stringed instrument they most often constituted a pitch that provided a tonal anchor, played on a low, open string. Tonic pedal tones are common opening and closing techniques, while dominant pedal tones often appear in the middle of a work or just before its final cadence. How do you go about determining harmonic content (and inversion!) above pedal tones, or are such analytic details unnecessary if we understand the pedal tone to indicate a prolongation of its attendant harmony?

28. Two Keyboard Fugues
(ca. 1740–42)

JOHANN SEBASTIAN BACH
(1685–1750)
❖

In the history of Western music, there is no more quintessential composer of fugue than J. S. Bach. The two works included here represent a tiny fraction of the genius he displayed in the genre. Examine the fugue from *Das wohltemperierte Klavier II* for its virtuosic use of stretto. And in the fugue from *Die Kunst der Fuge*—the collection Bach was working on just before his death—listen for the prodigious use of double invertible counterpoint.

FUGUE IN D MAJOR FROM *Das wohltemperierte Klavier II*, **BWV 874/2**

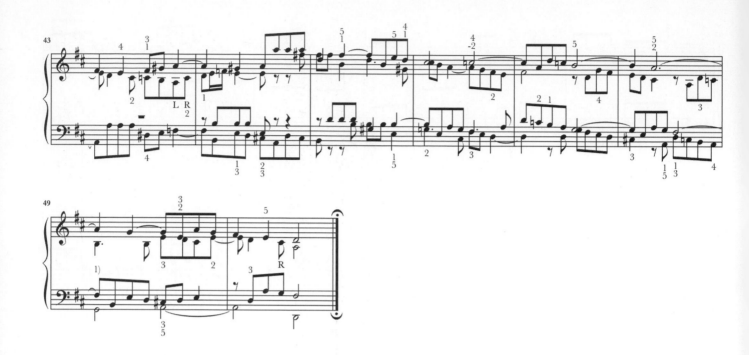

"CONTRAPUNCTUS X" FROM *Die Kunst der Fuge*, BWV 1080 (OFTEN PERFORMED IN ARRANGEMENT BY BRASS ENSEMBLES)

29. Gigue from French Suite No. 5 in G Major, BWV 816 (1722–25)

JOHANN SEBASTIAN BACH
(1685–1750)
❖

The Baroque-era dance forms found in the suite all have characteristic meters and rhythmic patterns. The gigue is a lively simple-triple-meter dance that features leaping figures; it is often the closing movement in a suite. Most suite movements are binary in form, being cast between a pair of repeat signs, or reprises. In Bach's hands, simple folk dances like the gigue can achieve a more learned sound through the use of imitative polyphonic lines. Some musicians use an analytic technique called "durational reduction" to help understand the lines, harmonies, and phrasing better to assist with performance decisions. See Larson (1983), who discusses the use of this technique in another Bach keyboard work and Burkhart (1994) for an essay on performance, rhythm, and meter in Bach's keyboard music.

Gigue

30. Solo Violin Sonata in G Minor, BWV 1001 *(1720)*

JOHANN SEBASTIAN BACH
(1685–1750)
❖

Baroque composers frequently conceived of single-line instrumental writing against a backdrop of a three- or four-part texture. What techniques does Bach use in these movements to create the sense of multiple voices? Compare this sonata (and the Bach cello suite movements) to the Telemann solo fantasies also included in this anthology. Do the two composers use essentially the same techniques in their single-line instrumental writing, or are there stylistic differences? Note also that many of Bach's compositions for single-line instruments have been transcribed for keyboard; it can be instructive to compare the arrangements to the originals. For some thoughts on performing Bach's solo violin works, see Lester (1999) and Brumbeloe (2000).

Adagio

Fuga: Allegro

31. Sarabande and Minuets from Cello Suite in G Major, BWV 1007 (ca. 1720)

JOHANN SEBASTIAN BACH
(1685–1750)
❖

The Baroque suite comprised a series of dance movements, with many—the sarabande and gigue, for instance—being standard, at least in eighteenth-century Germany. One technique for establishing a sense of unity across the various dance movements in the suite was to use similar forms and tonal plans. With this in mind, compare the Sarabande and the first Menuet. How are they similar in terms of tonicized key areas? Comparing the two Menuets, what (besides the change of mode) contributes to the sense of upward motion and levity in the first versus the sense of downward motion and gravity in the second? Finally, note that all three movements are binary forms. Trace their formal similarities and differences.

Bach strongly implies a three- or four-voice texture in his cello suites by using arpeggiation and polyphonic melody. These three movements come from the middle of the G Major cello suite. Though all three begin with an eight bar period for the first reprise, these opening statements are all distinct from one another. How? As you listen, try to determine the rate of harmonic rhythm; that is, how quickly do the implied harmonies tend to change? Is this rate of harmonic rhythm constant throughout each movement? Do the changes in harmonies tend to set up a metric pattern? If so, do you ever sense disruptions to the pattern, a syncopation or hemiola within the harmonic rhythm?

Finally note that, like the violin sonatas and partitas, the cello suites have also been arranged for other instruments, among them guitar, viola, and piano.

Sarabande

Menuet 1

Menuet 2

Menuet 1 da Capo

32. Menuetto I and II from Sonata in C Major, BWV 1033 (c. 1736), arr. for B♭ soprano saxophone

JOHANN SEBASTIAN BACH
(1685–1750)

❖

Bach's sonata BWV 1033 was written originally for flute and keyboard. Because the saxophone wasn't invented until the nineteenth century, saxophonists often arrange early works written for other wind instruments to be playable on alto or soprano saxophone. Most eighteenth-century performers of this work would have added ornamentation to the melodic line, especially when repeating sections of it. Do you think a saxophonist should adhere to this performance practice? If so, she might benefit from reading J. J. Quantz's *On Playing the Flute*, a treatise that examines, among other things, the question of melodic ornamentation.

Menuetto 1 da Capo

33. Larghetto from Concerto for Harp and Orchestra in B♭ Major, HWV 294 (1736)

GEORGE FRIDERIC HANDEL

(1685–1759)

❖

This Larghetto contains a number of sequential progressions. Where are they, and what kinds of sequences and elaborations does Handel use? Note especially the combination of a rising sequence followed by the flowering of a descending sequence in the solo harp, creating a beautiful climactic gesture in this movement.

34. Sonata in G Major for Violin and Basso Continuo, HWV 358 (c. 1707–10)

GEORGE FRIDERIC HANDEL
(1685–1759)

❖

When asked which time period within the common-practice period presents us with the most examples of music with ambiguous or problematic forms and/or tonalities, it is natural to think of the Romantic era. Slow movements in Baroque-era multimovement works, however, are often challenging in their own right. Take the Adagio from this sonata. What key is it in? Does it have a formal description? Is it even a "complete" piece (whatever that may mean), or does it constitute only transitional, connective tissue between the first and third movements? What implications do the answers to these questions have on performance decisions?

Adagio

35. Sonata in C Minor for Oboe and Basso Continuo, HWV 366 (c. 1711–12)

GEORGE FRIDERIC HANDEL
(1685–1759)

❖

SLOW

As we have noted at other points in this anthology, it can be easy to forget that the relationship between analysis and performance is a two-way street. True, analysis can often inform performance decisions, but the converse is also often the case. Play through the melody line of the Largo from Handel's oboe sonata. Does performing this music make it easier to speak analytically about phrasing and melodic organization in this movement? Do your musical intuitions seem to align with how you might speak about this music analytically? Why or why not?

Note that this work has been arranged for piccolo trumpet and piano.

Bourrée anglaise — Allegro

36. Allegro vigoroso from Sonata in C Minor (1739?), arr. for harp

GIOVANNI BATTISTA PESCETTI
(1704–66)

How important is it, when performing an arrangement, to look at the original score? There are, after all, often technical and musical compromises that need to be made when arranging music originally intended for one instrument for another. In this regard, since it could be argued that the composer's original intent (if it is something we value in performance) has already been violated by the arranger, performers might consider a comparison of arrangement with original as an exercise in interpretive decision making. In fact, many performers feel no compunction in amending an arrangement to arrive at what might be a more satisfying realization of the music based on the original score.

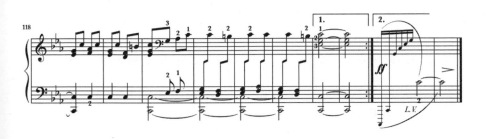

37. Allegretto from Sonata for Flute and Keyboard in G major, H 564, "Hamburg" (1786)

CARL PHILIPP EMANUEL BACH
(1714–88)
❖

C.P.E. Bach's so-called Hamburg sonata draws its name from the city in which it was composed. After serving in the court of the flute-playing Kaiser "Frederick the Great" of Prussia in Potsdam (near Berlin), Bach eventually succeeded the most celebrated composer of Baroque-era Germany, Georg Philip Telemann, as Kapellmeister at Hamburg. His sonata is an early example of sonata form, one in which its relation to the simpler rounded binary form from whence it emerged is quite clear. Notice, as well, the long-breathed opening flute melody, an artifact of the *empfindsamer Stil* ("sensitive style") Bach championed.

38. Allegro from String Quartet in D Minor, Op. 76, No. 2, "Quinten" *(1797)*

JOSEPH HAYDN
(1732–1809)

❖

Joseph Haydn's string quartets are remarkable not only for their expressive range but also for their formal and tonal innovations. For Haydn, the string quartet was a compositional laboratory of sorts, one that was quintessentially experimental. The "Quinten" quartet, so named because of its prevalent motto, is a case in point; its first movement is a unique example of sonata form for any number of reasons. What might some of these be?

39. Moderato from Piano Sonata in G Minor, Hob. 44 *(1788)*

JOSEPH HAYDN
(1732–1809)

❖

Much Classic-era music presents a kaleidoscope of shifting topics, or topos: musical tropes and gestures that evoke everything from marches to dances, singing, learned counterpoint, fanfares, and chorales. Many scholars—among them Leonard Meyer, Robert Hatten, Lawrence Kramer, and Michael Klein—have explored how topics contribute to a sense of musical meaning. Can you hear a succession of such topics in this movement? How might each of them—and the changes from one to another—suggest performance interpretation?

40. Andante from Symphony No. 72 in D Major, Hob. I:72 (1781)

JOSEPH HAYDN
(1732–1809)
❖

Joseph Haydn is widely considered to be the father of the symphony. Many of his symphonic movements, like his string quartets, are highly experimental, but this piece is a model of clarity, balance, and restraint. Its primary interest lies in what Haydn does with orchestration and the cohesive elaboration of the melody line in each variation. It is also an excellent work to use for beginning score reading and for playing at the keyboard. Try first to play the basic two-part harmony of the Thema; then recognize how this same structure is present when you attempt the sixth variation, an exemplar of Classic-era orchestration in which the string section makes up the harmonic core of the ensemble, the winds serve as soloists and doublings, and the brass and percussion reinforce the tonic and dominant harmonies. Despite the simplicity of many theme-and-variation movements from the eighteenth and nineteenth centuries, like this one, other composers were able to adapt to artistic expressions that were subtler or more forceful. Compare this variation set to the ones later in this anthology by Beethoven and Arban.

Thema
Andante

41. *Ave Verum Corpus*, K. 618 *(1791)*

WOLFGANG AMADEUS MOZART
(1756–91)

The text of Mozart's late motet *Ave Verum Corpus* is biblical. Its translation runs as follows:

Hail, true Body
born of the Virgin Mary:
truly suffered, sacrificed
on the cross for humankind;
whose pierced side
flowed with water and blood:
May it be for us a foretaste
in the trial of death.

Translation: Anonymous

Although this work is often performed by high-school choral groups with piano, the piano part in the score below is actually a transcription; the original calls for string orchestra. As you examine this work, how do the cadences and chromatic passages seem to relate to the text setting?

Adagio

42. Menuetto and Trio from Wind Serenade in C Minor, K. 388 *(1782 or 1783)*

WOLFGANG AMADEUS MOZART
(1756–91)
❖

Mozart's reputation for musical genius is borne out in this short movement. The menuetto includes a canon at the octave while the trio contains a pair of canons in inversion! When studying this work, pay attention to how Mozart structures the canons—including how and where he breaks them in the menuetto movement—so as to conform to the tonal and thematic norms of Classic-era binary forms.

Note that Mozart arranged this music for string quintet in the third movement of K. 406/516b.

43. Allegro aperto from Concerto for Flute (or Oboe) and Orchestra in D (C) Major, K. 314 *(1778)*

WOLFGANG AMADEUS MOZART
(1756–91)

❖

Textbooks often characterize Classic-era concerti as "double exposition" forms—that is, sonata forms in which there are two expositions, a first, non-modulatory exposition for the orchestra and a second, modulatory exposition for the soloist. There are certainly many examples that conform to this model, but many more do not. Old paradigms of ritornello form from the Baroque era and inventive exploitations of the tension between soloist and orchestra often combine with elements of sonata form in Mozart's concerti. Does that seem to be the case here?

44. Duett für Zwei Violinen, "Der Spiegel," attrib. K. Anh. 284^{dd}

WOLFGANG AMADEUS MOZART
(1756–91)

❖

This work, attributed to Mozart, belongs to a long tradition of lighthearted eighteenth-century parlor music written to entertain amateur musicians with games, puzzles, humorous texts, and the like. The gimmick in this work is readily apparent. Given that both parts are read in treble clef, why might G major make the most sense as the tonic key of choice?

Allegro

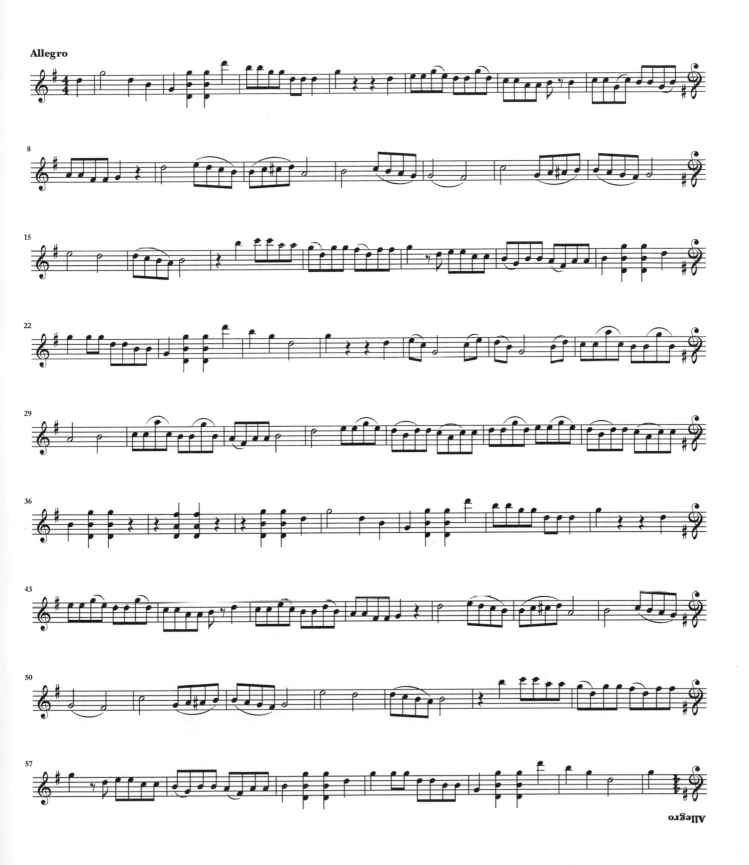

45. Adagio from Quartet for Flute and Strings in D Major, K. 285 *(1777)*

WOLFGANG AMADEUS MOZART

(1756–91)

❖

Accompanists are commonly instructed to follow the phrasing and other musical decisions of the soloists with whom they play. In this movement it is clear that the flute is the lead melodic voice and the pizzicato strings play the role of accompanist (standing in for a harp, as it were). But does this mean the string players have little say about shaping the musical performance? What perspective might an accompanist have on the music that could be of value to the soloist in interpretive decision making?

46. Rondeau Allegro from Quartet for Oboe and Strings in F Major, K. 370
(1781)

WOLFGANG AMADEUS MOZART
(1756–91)

❖

The third movement from Mozart's oboe quintet may be the first work of common-practice tonal art music to feature two notated meters operative at the same time; see mm. 95*ff*. What is the immediate, local effect of this metric conflict, and what role does the section play in the form as a whole?

47. Rondo Allegretto from Quintet for Piano and Winds in E♭ Major, K. 452 (1784)

WOLFGANG AMADEUS MOZART
(1756–91)
❖

Shortly after completing this work, Mozart wrote a letter to his father stating that he thought this quintet was the best thing he had ever composed. The work began life as a piano concerto, but Mozart later changed his mind and decided to make it a chamber work. Nevertheless, elements of the concerto remain. The cadenza, for instance, is unusual for a chamber work from this time period. Why do you think Mozart wrote it out rather than leaving it up to the performers? Also, where do you think the cadential $^6_4$ that opens the cadenza resolves? Scholar Robert Gjerdingen points to this cadenza as a concatenation of galant-era schemata (i.e., patterns).[6] Many of these are sequential in nature. How many can you find? Do you hear any nested sequences?

Note that this work has been arranged for piano and saxophone quartet.

---

[6]Gjerdingen (2007), 447–51.

Rondo: Allegretto

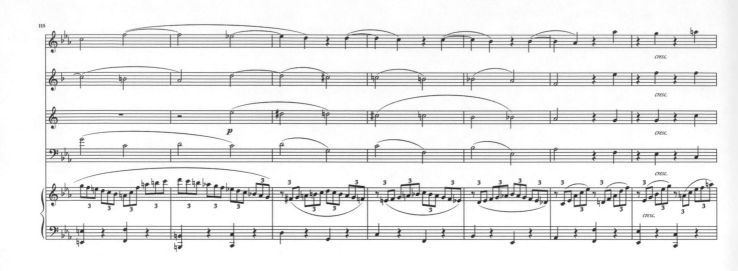

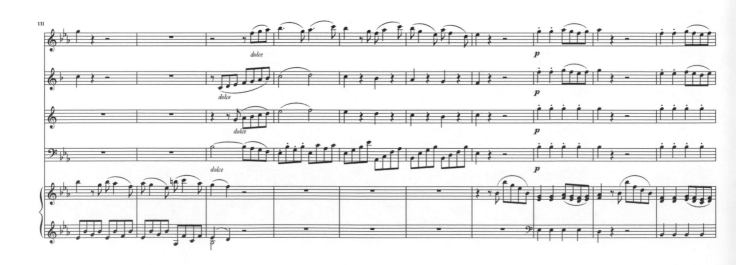

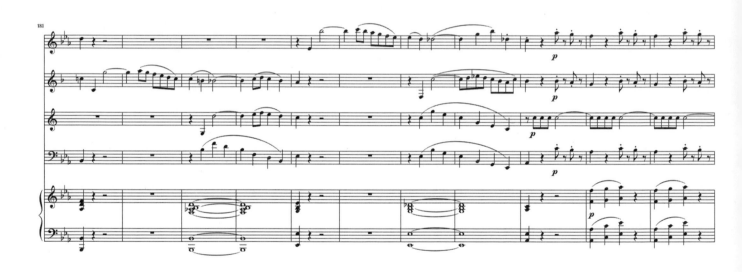

48. Allegro maestoso from Piano Sonata in A Minor, K. 310 *(1778)*

WOLFGANG AMADEUS MOZART

(1756–91)

❖

Mozart wrote relatively few works in the minor mode; most are expressively powerful.[7] This work, a clear exemplar of sonata form, contains some interesting sequential passages. Look, for example, at mm. 6–7 and 58–70. How does the later passage compare with the nested sequence in the cadenza to the Quintet for Piano and Winds, K. 452? Listen, also, for cadences throughout. Which are true points of closure and should be emphasized as such? How might the others be performed? For some thoughts on these and other questions relating hypermetric and tonal structure to performance decisions, see Beach (1987).[88]

[7]For a list of many of these minor-mode works, their typical expressive uses in Mozart's hands, and a grounding of Mozart's usage in contemporary music theory, see Wheelock (1993).
[8]For a clear introduction to the concept of hypermeter, see Krebs (2004).

49. Scherzo from Symphony No. 7 in A Major
(1811–12)

LUDWIG VAN BEETHOVEN
(1770–1827)
❖

Beethoven's seventh symphony departs from tonal and formal norms of the period in a number of ways. The third movement, for example, in is a key distantly related to the tonic. (For a fascinating account of many of this symphony's idiosyncrasies and how they tie into a large-scale plan, see Gauldin (1991).) Beethoven's symphonic scherzi provide many clear examples of both regular hypermeter and hypermetric disruption. Can you find the points of hypermetric disruption in this work? Is there any logic to their placement?

Note that Beethoven himself arranged this work for wind octet.

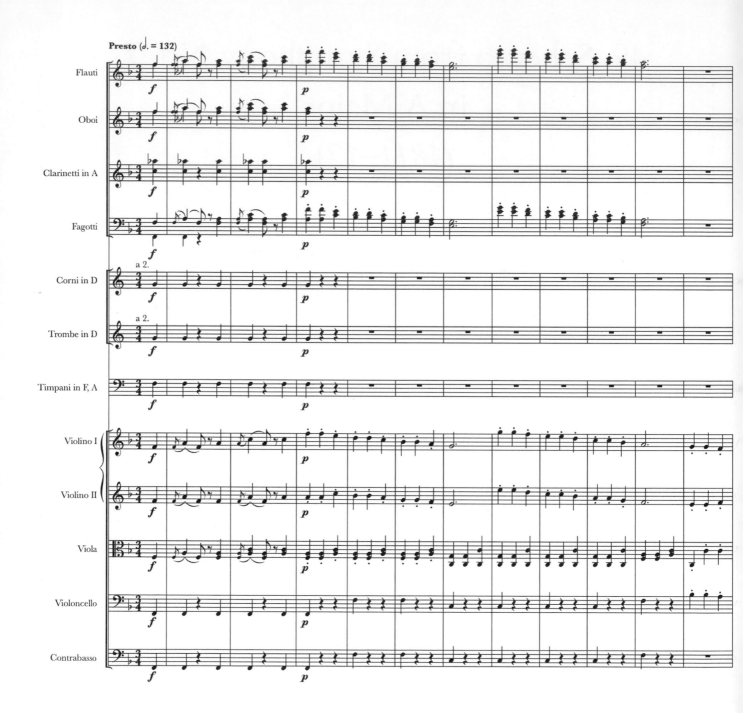

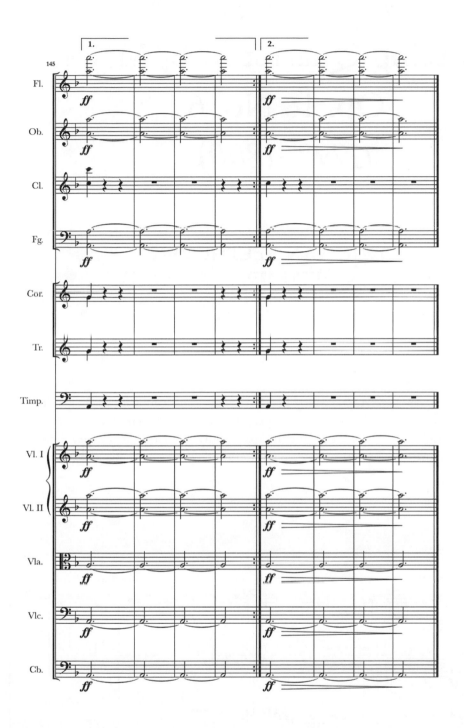

50. String Quartet in B♭ Major, Op. 18 No. 6 (1798–1800)

LUDWIG VAN BEETHOVEN

(1770–1827)

❖

These two movements demonstrate the young Beethoven experimenting with meter and form. In the Scherzo, how does Beethoven create the experience of "shadow meter," or two conflicting meters whose downbeats are an eighth-note apart? How does the *Malinconia* material interact with the following Allegretto to create an unorthodox musical shape and expressive statement?

La Malinconia
Questo pezzo si deve trattare colla più gran delicatezza

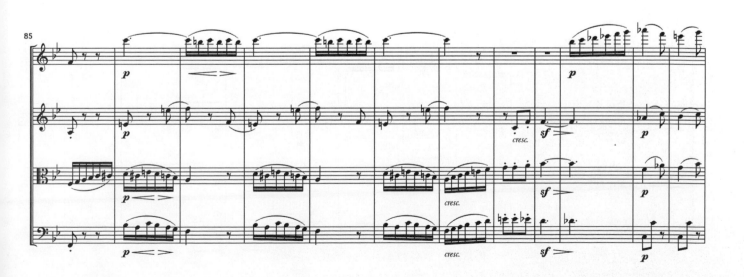

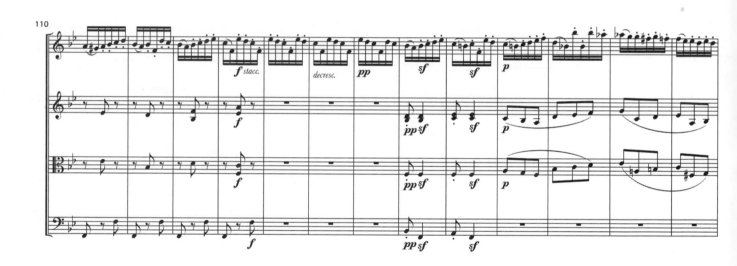

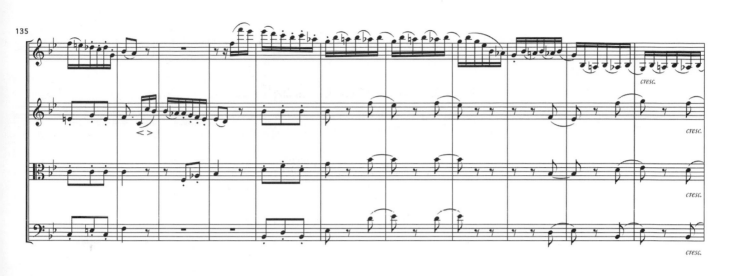

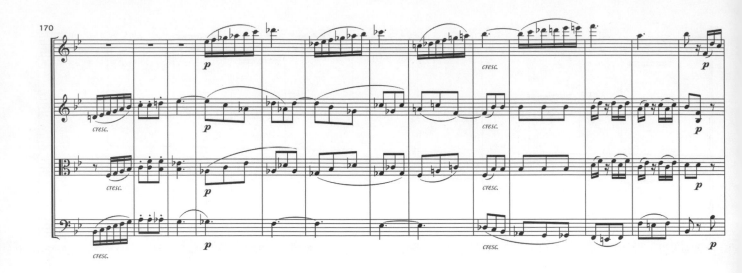

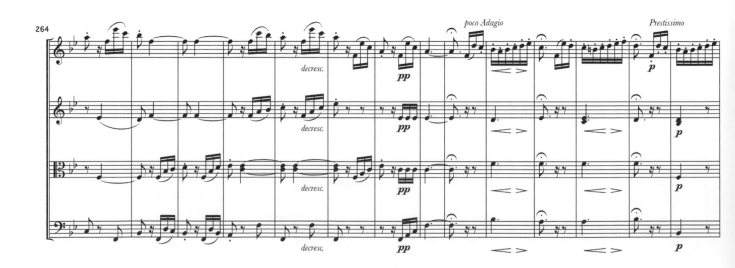

51. Adagio cantabile from Trio in C Major for Two Oboes and English Horn, Op. 87
(1795?)

LUDWIG VAN BEETHOVEN
(1770–1827)

❖

This is a charming, but little-known, work from Beethoven's early period. Study it especially for the variety of nested formal paradigms Beethoven uses and the manner in which he varies recurring material.

52. Allegro Moderato from Sonata for Horn or Cello and Piano in F Major, Op. 17 *(1800)*

LUDWIG VAN BEETHOVEN
(1770–1827)

❖

This is an early work of Beethoven's, existing in two versions. Despite melodic differentiation between the cello and horn versions, the piano part—and thus the harmonic structure—remains the same. Some of the differences can certainly be attributed to the limitations of the hand horn; this work was written before the valved horn came into existence. Are all the differences so easily explained, though? Do they affect the performance of the piano part? And might a horn player using a modern instrument elect to play the cello version rather than the original version for horn?

53. Allegro from Sonata for Violin and Piano in F Major, Op. 24 ("Spring"; 1800–01)

LUDWIG VAN BEETHOVEN
(1770–1827)
❖

Notice that the title for this piece is rightly "Sonata for Violin and Piano," rather than the oft-cited "Violin Sonata." The latter moniker implies that the violin is the solo instrument and the piano mere accompaniment. Although this soloist-with-accompaniment arrangement was common in Romantic-era music, many sonatas by composers such as Mozart and Beethoven demonstrate that piano, and in this case, violin share the role of thematic exposition and melodic foregrounding. Unsurprisingly, the opening movement of this work is cast in sonata form. Examine, however, the tonal areas of the exposition. What is unusual about Beethoven's choice of keys in the exposition and at the end of the development?

54. Allegro con brio from Piano Sonata in C Major, Op. 53 (*"Waldstein"; 1804*)

LUDWIG VAN BEETHOVEN
(1770–1827)

❖

Among music scholars, Beethoven's "Waldstein" sonata is well known for its innovative formal-tonal plan. Examine the exposition carefully. How do the thematic content and modulation scheme in the exposition conform to the norms of sonata composition, and how do they differ? When this material returns in the recapitulation, how does Beethoven handle it?

55. Gesangvoll, mit innigster Empfindung. Andante molto cantabile ed espressivo from Piano Sonata in E Major, Op. 109 *(1820)*

LUDWIG VAN BEETHOVEN
(1770–1827)

❖

As the performance instructions in the title above might suggest, this set of variations by Beethoven traverses a wide range of expressive states. By what technical means does Beethoven accomplish this, and how does his compositional technique in this regard differ from that used in the variation sets by Haydn and Arban included in this anthology?

Var. III: Allegro vivace

Var. IV: Etwas langsamer als das Thema

56. Lento–Allegro Moderato from Quintet for Winds in E♭ Major, Op. 88, No. 2

ANTON REICHA
(1770–1836)

The origins of the woodwind quintet—an ensemble comprising flute, oboe, clarinet, horn, and bassoon—are murky. Few would contest the assertion that the ensemble sprang from the *Harmonie* and other groups of wind instruments favored at German and Austrian courts in the eighteenth century. But the invention of this specific quintet instrumentation could rightly go to one of three composers: Giuseppe Cambini, Antonio Rosetti, or Nikolaus Schmitt. They were followed by the slightly younger Franz Danzi and Anton Reicha. Many of the early works composed by these men are still considered important in the woodwind quintet repertory even though the bulk of the music written for this ensemble comes from the twentieth century. How do the instruments in this ensemble function relative to those in works written for other chamber groups such as the string quartet?

57. "Liebeszauber" Op. 13, No. 3 (1807)

CARL MARIA VON WEBER

(1786–1826)

❖

Considered by some to be a second-rate composer, it is obvious from this example that Weber's talents in song writing pale in comparison to the genius of, say, Schubert. When musicians make comparisons about the music of two composers, though, they rarely divulge the structural components of the music upon which at least some of these judgments are made. What is it about harmony, form, text setting, or other characteristics that might lead one to make such an invidious comparison with Schubert?

Lass, look me in the face!
Do not blink your coquettish eyes!
Lass, mark what I say!
Speak to me when I ask!
Speak fully in my face!
Do not blink your coquettish eyes!

You're not ugly, that is true;
Your pretty eyes are clear and blue;
Your cheeks and mouth are like sweet figs;
Ach! About your bosom I will remain silent!
You are lovely, sweetheart, that is true.
You are lovely, manifestly.

But you're lovely only here and there!
You are not a queen;
Not the Queen of the Beauties.
Worthy alone of that crown.
Lovely here and lovely there!
Lacking much that makes one a queen.

A hundred beauties, surely,
A hundred, a hundred! were to be found,
Were to be eager,
To steal your beauty from you by comparison.
A hundred beauties were to be found;
A hundred triumph over you.

Still you foster your royal rights
Over your true slave:
The royal privilege in your heart,
Quick to bliss, quick to pain.
Death and life, your royal privilege,
You take these from your true slave!

58. Allegro moderato from Sonata in A Minor for Piano and Arpeggione, D. 821
(1824)

FRANZ SCHUBERT
(1797–1828)
❖

The arpeggione was a six-stringed, fretted instrument not unlike the viola da gamba. Invented by a Viennese guitar maker, it enjoyed an extremely short span of time as a common part of musical life in the 1820s. Nevertheless, during this time period Schubert wrote a splendid sonata for it, now usually performed by viola, cello, or trombone.

59. Allegro from Piano Sonata in A Major, D. 959
(1828)

FRANZ SCHUBERT
(1797–1828)

❖

Robert Hatten makes an interesting argument about Schubert's sonata form in this movement: namely that it is innovative for its use of resonance and gesture rather than for its motives, themes, and key areas (see Hatten, 1993). What do you think? If this kind of analytic approach interests you, look into how the resonant effect of the opening theme of this first movement plays out in the three remaining movements.

60. "Erster Verlust" (1815)

FRANZ SCHUBERT
(1797–1828)

❖

This song, like Schubert's "Erlkönig," was written early in the composer's career. Both are testament to his prodigious dramatic talent. The artistic merits of "Erster Verlust," however, are perhaps subtler than those in the other work. Pay special attention to the relationship between the text (by Goethe) and the sense of local tonic key. Does this song have one clear tonic key? If so, what is it, and why? Would your answer change if the last bar of the work were omitted? For further commentary on the relationship between tonic key and performance, see Stein and Spillman (1996), 122–23.

> Ah, who will bring back those beautiful days—
> those days of first love?
> Ah, who will bring back even just one hour
> of that lovely time?
>
> Lonely, I nourish my wound
> and with constantly renewed laments,
> I mourn my lost happiness.
>
> Ah, who will bring back those beautiful days—
> that lovely time?

Translation: Emily Ezust

Sehr langsam, wehmüthig

Ach, wer bringt die schö - nen Ta - ge, je - ne Ta - ge der er - sten Lie - be, ach, wer bringt nur ei - ne Stun - de

pp   *fp*   *cresc.*

je - ner hol - den Zeit zu - rück! Ein - sam nähr' ich mei - ne Wun - de, und mit stets er - neu - ter Kla - ge traur'

pp   *mf*

ich um's ver - lor' - ne Glück. Ach, wer bringt die schö - nen Ta - ge, wer je - ne hol - de Zeit zu - rück!

pp   *fp*   *p*   *pp*

61. "Der Neugierige" from *Die schöne Müllerin* *(1823)*

FRANZ SCHUBERT
(1797–1828)

"Der Neugierige," the sixth song of Schubert's beloved *Die schöne Müllerin* cycle, is a reflective reverie; the poem's protagonist asks whether or not the young woman he loves feels similarly. The brook he addresses in the poem (by Wilhelm Müller) is with him throughout the cycle and frequently serves as a mute sounding board for the young man's thoughts and feelings. Listen to the opening gesture in the piano's right hand. Although one might explain the high G# in melodic terms as a neighbor to F#, that pitch does not follow immediately in the same register. The significance of this missing F# relative to the remainder of the song's text and tonal structure constitutes the heart of David Beach's analysis of this song (see Beach, 1998). What implications might Beach's observations have for performance? Think also about questions of harmonic rhythm, texture, and tempo choices in this song. For some observations on these, see Stein and Spillman (1996), 77 and 173.

Note that this work has been arranged for other performing forces, among them voice and guitar, and flute and piano.

> I ask no flower.
> I ask no star.
> None of them can tell me
> what I so greatly want to hear.
>
> I am, after all, no gardener,
> and the stars are too high.
> I will ask my brook
> whether my heart has lied to me.

O little brook of my love,
how silent you are today!
I want to know just one thing,
one little word, over and over again.

One word is Yes,
the other is No.
The two little words contain
the whole world for me.

O little brook of my love,
how strange you are today!
I'll tell no one else:
tell me, little brook, does she love me?

Translation: Youens (1997), 41

62. "Il faut partir" from
La Fille du Régiment
(1840)

GAETANO DONIZETTI
(1797–1848)
❖

Although Donizetti's opera *La Fille du Régiment* is about love, and especially sex, "Il faut partir," the scene in which the musical protagonist Marie says goodbye to a regiment of soldiers, is ripe for parody because it captures none of the sexual tension inherent in the drama. Rather, a bunch of pouty-faced soldiers listen to Marie as she sings sweetly and innocently about how she'll miss the pleasure of their company. The music is plaintive and repetitive, and the emotional nuance of the situation is limited to rather hackneyed uses of the Neapolitan sonority and modulation to parallel keys. Compare this music with Verdi's setting of a similar scene in *La Traviata*.

   Note that this opera was written in France, to a French libretto. Thus the title is most often reproduced in French. Donizetti later crafted an Italian-language version.

63. Piano Trio in D Major, Op. 11
(1846)

FANNY MENDELSSOHN HENSEL
(1805–47)
❖

Like Wolfgang and Nannerl Mozart, Fanny and Felix Mendelssohn were musical siblings trained from early childhood as prodigies. Both Mendelssohns composed in adulthood, and both, sadly, died young. As you listen to these movements from Fanny Mendelssohn Hensel's piano trio, is there anything in the music's structure or affective content that suggests it was written by a woman? The question may strike us as strange today, but in the nineteenth century women who wrote music often faced a catch-22: those whose music didn't resemble the "strong," Germanic, masculine works of composers such as Beethoven were deemed lesser, obviously feminine composers. Those like English composer Ethel Smyth, however, whose works did emulate what Western Europe considered masculine traits were accused of over-reaching the natural abilities of their gender!

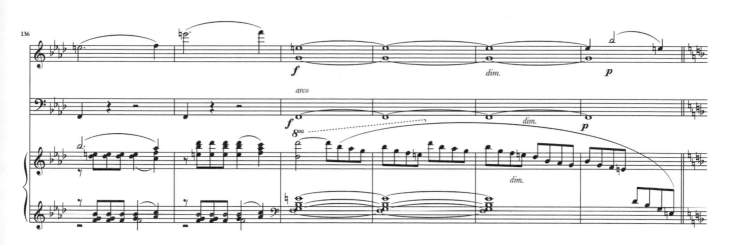

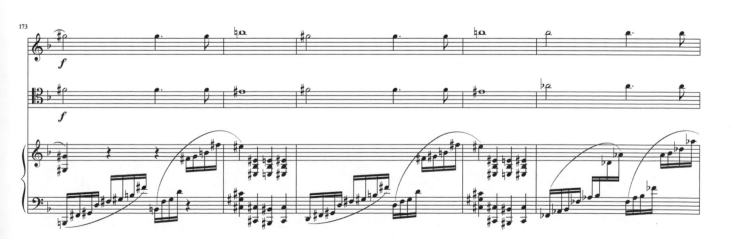

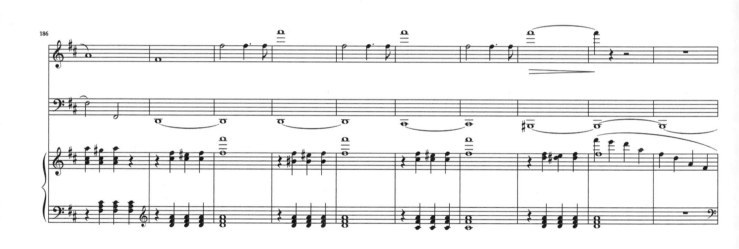

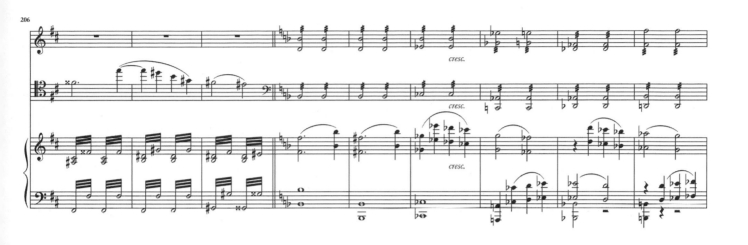

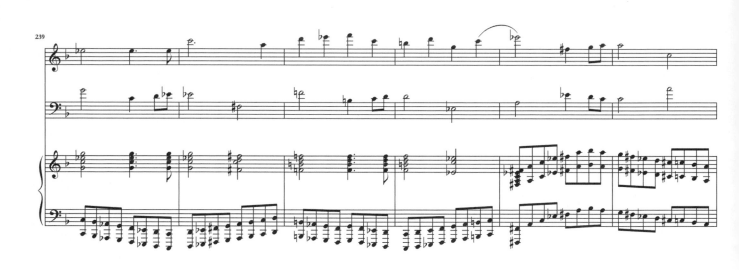

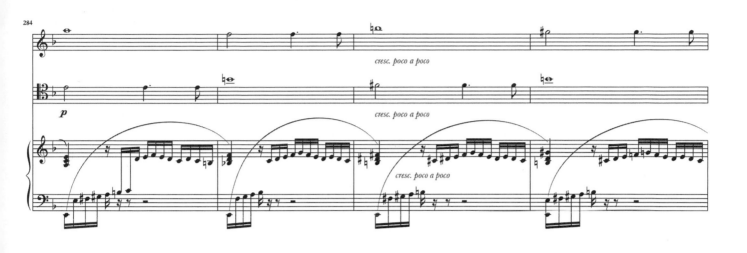

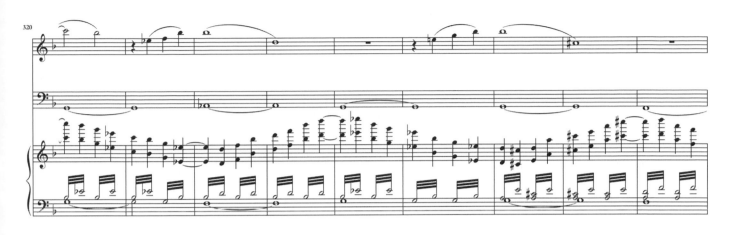

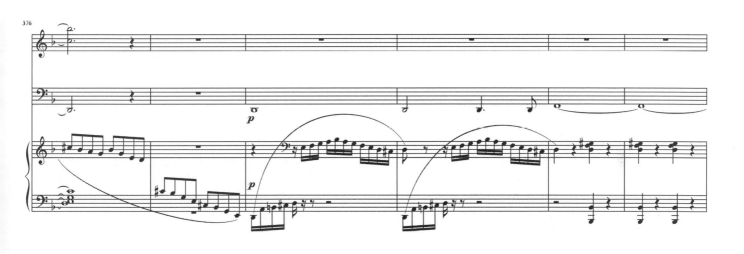

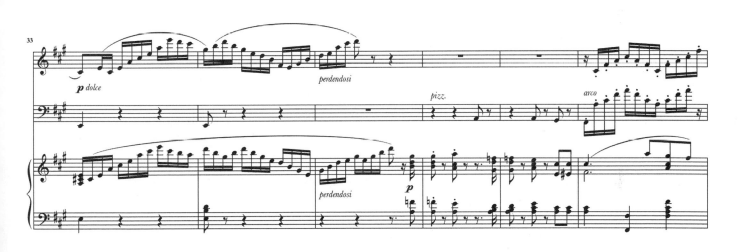

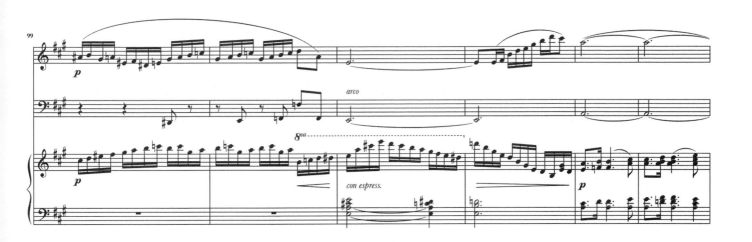

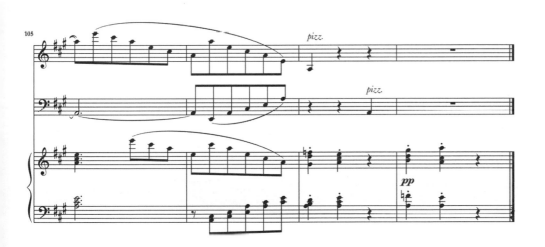

64. Two Songs Without Words from Op. 62

FELIX MENDELSSOHN
(1809–47)
❖

Both of these piano works are called songs, though there is no singer and no text. Listen closely to the texture, melodic line, and phrasing. Compare them to the many lieder in this anthology. What is there about these piano pieces that seems songlike? If there is an evocation of a vocal line, are other, accompanimental, instrumental sounds created as well?

Note that these works have been arranged for other performing forces, among them violin and piano, flute and piano, and chorus.

NO. 1 (1844)

NO. 6 (1842)

65. Two Preludes from Op. 28
(1838–39)

FRYDERYK CHOPIN
(1810–49)

❖

William Rothstein's 2005 article on Chopin's A♭ Major Prelude identifies an *Ur*-rhythm made up of five eighth-notes whose final member arrives on the downbeat. Identification of this end-accented gesture initiates discussion of performance decisions concerning rubato and downward versus upward motion. Can the same approach be extrapolated fruitfully when thinking about the considerably faster and briefer D Major Prelude?[9]

NO. 17 IN A♭ MAJOR

[9]See Schachter (1994) for an analysis of this piece concerned specifically with performance issues.

NO. 5 IN D MAJOR

66. Fantasiestück, Op. 73, No. 3 for Clarinet and Piano
(1849)

ROBERT SCHUMANN
(1810–56)

❖

This charming work is filled with accented dissonances on the downbeats. Some of them resolve down (as expected) while others resolve up. Is there any harmonic, motivic, or expressive reason for these differing resolutions? Might a distinction be made in performance? If so, how?

Note that this work has been arranged for other solo instruments with piano, among them oboe, horn, bassoon, and baritone saxophone.

67. *Märchenbild*, Op. 113, No. 1
(1851)

ROBERT SCHUMANN

(1810–56)

❖

Where is the cadence that concludes this work's tonal journey? That is, at what point do you hear the conclusive return to the tonic harmony? Could you argue for more than one point? Try performing the tonic arrivals in a variety of places. Does performing them help you decide which seems the best candidate?

68. "Widmung," Op. 25, No. 1 *(1840)*

ROBERT SCHUMANN
(1810–56)

❖

Robert Schumann wrote "Widmung" ("Dedication") in 1840—the so-called year of song—when lieder inspired by his marriage to Clara Wieck poured out of his pen at an amazing rate. Noteworthy in this song is the Ab-E chromatic key relationship. Do you think it is motivated by the text (by Rückert)? If so, how? Note also the falling Db-C melodic figure on "lebe" ("live") in m. 7. This figure returns in a beautiful new context across mm. 25–27, spanning the seam between the end of the E-major middle section and the return to Ab. This is but one repeated musical figure in the song. Others may assist in the singer's choice of tempo and phrasing. See Stein and Spillman (1996), 70–72 and 75–76.

You my soul, you my heart,
you my bliss, o you my pain,
you the world in which I live;
you my heaven, in which I float,
o you my grave, into which
I eternally cast my grief.
You are rest, you are peace,
you are bestowed upon me from heaven.
That you love me makes me worthy of you;
your gaze transfigures me;
you raise me lovingly above myself,
my good spirit, my better self!

Translation: Emily Ezust

Innig, lebhaft

Du mei-ne See - le, du mein Herz, du mei-ne Wonn',___ O du mein

Schmerz, du mei-ne Welt,___ in der ich le - be, mein Him - mel du,___ dar-ein ich schwe - be, o du mein

ritard.

Grab, in das hin-ab ich e - - wig mei-nen Kum - - - mer gab!

Du bist die Ruh', du bist___ der Frie - den; du bist vom

69. Marsch funebre from Concertino in E♭ Major for Trombone and Orchestra, Op. 4 *(1837)*

FERDINAND DAVID

(1810–73)

❖

The idea of the musical topic (or *topos*) appeared earlier in this anthology, with regard to Haydn's g-minor piano sonata. Such topics, common in much Classic (and later) music, often rely on a number of characteristics for their identities. One of the more prevalent topics employed by composers in the nineteenth century was the funeral march. What musical attributes lead us to identify this topos, and are they used to good effect in this movement here?

70. *Die Trauer-Gondel* No. 1
(*La Lugubre Gondola; 1882–85*)

FRANZ LISZT
(1811–86)
❖

This work, and another of the same title, were written to evoke a funereal procession in which a gondola on the Grand Canal of Venice bears the remains of the recently deceased Richard Wagner. *Die Trauer-Gondol* stands among a number of other experimental Liszt piano pieces that seem to foreshadow some of the tonality-abrogating trends that swept Europe decades later. In this work, what sonority does Liszt use to depict the mysterious scene, and what are the ramifications of its usage on the sense of tonality in this work as a whole?

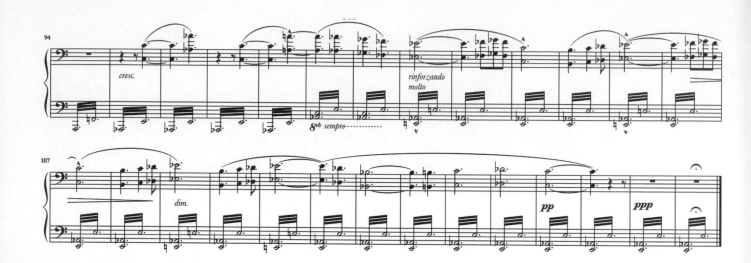

71. Elsa's Procession to the Cathedral from *Lohengrin* Act II, scene iv *(1848)*

RICHARD WAGNER
(1813–83)

❖

This music comes to us—along with the more famous "Wedding March"—from Wagner's opera *Lohengrin*. Many wind and brass players will be familiar with it, since a number of arrangements have been made for concert band and brass ensembles. The score, replete with extended instruments and voices, is characteristic of large, Romantic-era orchestral works. Reading multiple clefs and transposing instruments makes this type of score among the most challenging to decipher. Even though piano-vocal reductions for Wagner's operas are readily available, reading from the original score is a worthwhile endeavor. As you study this one, pay special attention to how modulations are achieved and what Wagner does with phrase rhythm.

72. "Ah fors'è lui" from *La Traviata* (1852)

GIUSEPPE VERDI
(1813–1901)

❖

In this final scene of Act One of *La Traviata*, Violetta is torn over whether to remain free or to give her heart to Alfredo. In "Ah fors'è lui" ("Ah, perhaps he is the one") Violetta makes her decision and bids farewell to her freewheeling lifestyle, in particular the male companionship that the opening act makes it clear she has enjoyed. Verdi sets this scene in a hilarious parody to Marie's innocent farewell to the soldiers in Donizetti's "Il faut partir" from *La fille du regiment* by drawing on many musical elements used in the earlier selection. What are they? Can you hear how the music from "Il faut partir" is humorously placed in a context that is highly sexually suggestive in *La Traviata*?

mul - ti   go - dea so - ven - te pin - ge - re   de' suoi co - lo - ri - oc - cul - ti, de' suoi col - lo - rioc - cul - ti! Lui, che mo - de - sto - e vi - gi -

A me, fan - ciul - la, un can - di - do   e tre-pi-do de - si – re,   e tre-pi-do de - si - re,   quest' ef - fi - giò dol - cis - si - mo

sig-nor dell' av-ve - ni — re,   sig-nor dell' av-ve - ni – re,   quan-do ne' cie-li–il rag - gio di sua bel-tà ve – de – a,   e tut-ta me pa - sce - a

ver - - so, del-l'u - - ni - ver-so-in-te - - ro, mi - ste - ri - o - - so,

mi - ste-ri-o-so,al - te - ro, cro - ce, cro-ce-è de - li - zia, cro-ce-è de - li - zia, de-li-zia-al cor! cro-ce-è de - li - zia, de-li-zia-al

73. "Liebst du um Schönheit" (1841)

CLARA WIECK SCHUMANN
(1819–96)

❖

This work appeared as part of a collection published by Robert Schumann. All twelve lieder were poems by Rückert set to music. Robert and his wife, Clara, both contributed to the collection, but because of the gender biases present in nineteenth-century European publication, all the songs were published under Robert's name. This lied, by Clara, features a modified strophic form. Trace the modifications from strophe to strophe. Are the modifications harmonic or textural in nature? Does there seem to be any connection to the text?

If you love for beauty,
O love me not!
Love instead the sun,
For she has golden hair!

If you love for youth,
O love me not!
Love instead the spring
Who is young each year!

If you love for riches,
O love me not!
Love instead the mermaid
Who has many glistening pearls!

If you love for love,
Oh yes, then love me!
Love me always;
For I will always love you!

Liebst du um Lie - be, o ja mich lie - be! Liebst du um Lie - be, o ja mich lie - be,

lie - be mich im-mer, dich lieb' ich im - - - mer dar!

74. Nocturno for Horn and Piano, Op. 7 *(1867)*

FRANZ STRAUSS

(1822–1905)

❖

This lovely work was penned by Franz Strauss, accounted by Richard Wagner as the best hornist in Europe. (Though Strauss disliked Wagner, he consented to play in the composer's *Ring*-cycle orchestra.) Compositionally, Franz was eclipsed by his son, Richard, who throughout his oeuvre explored the technical and musical limits of the horn. Many of Richard's early works, though, betray a Classical sensibility audible here in his father's work. How do you hear harmony and form operating? Would you deem their usage more "Classic" or "Romantic," or are such distinctions of little value when preparing a work for performance?

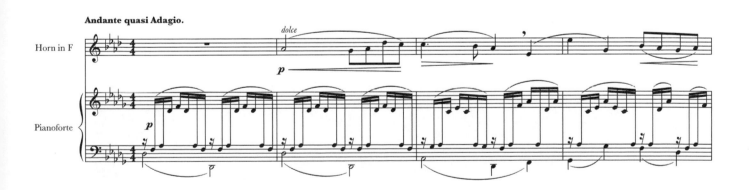

75. Two Spiritual Motets (1885)

ANTON BRUCKNER
(1824–96)

❖

Anton Bruckner was considered a musical conservative. Though he was heavily influenced by radical trends in harmony propagated by Richard Wagner, his compositional vantage point often looked backward rather than forward. Bruckner's strong Catholic faith and reliance on established genres—such as the symphony and motet—distinguished him from other composers of the day. His theorizing, too, tended to be traditional; the focus on harmony rather than line in his writings translates as well into much of his music, which is often characterized as being of great harmonic richness but lacking in melody and counterpoint. The two spiritual motets here display both Bruckner's harmonic ingenuity—note the many chromatic modulations and how they are achieved—and his musical conservatism, exhibited by the motet genre and his use of Latin chant tunes. Compare Bruckner's four-part settings to the Bach chorales in score 25. In terms of texture, there are many similarities. In terms of structure, though, they are worlds apart.

"TOTA PULCHRA ES"
You are all beautiful, Mary.
The stain of original sin is not in you.
You are Jerusalem's glory.
You are Israel's joy.
You bring honor to our people.
You bring council for our sins.
Oh, Mary, Mary!
Wisest virgin.
Most merciful mother.
Pray on our behalf.
Intercede on our behalf
With our Lord, Jesus Christ.

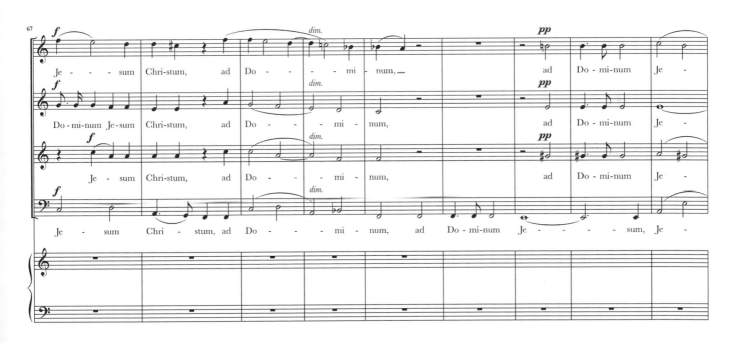

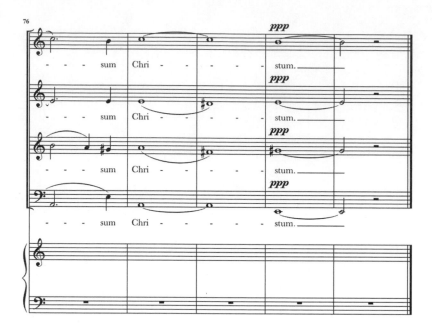

"VIRGA JESSE"

The branch from Jesse blossoms:
a Virgin begets God and man in one:
God restores peace,
Reconciling within Himself the least and greatest.
Alleluia

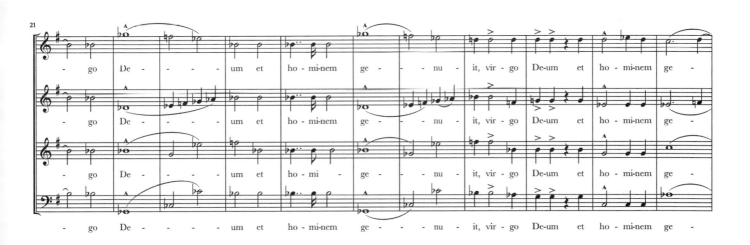

76. Andante Moderato from Caprice et Variations for E♭ Alto Saxophone and Piano
(1881)

JEAN-BAPTISTE ARBAN
(1825–89)
❖

Jean-Baptiste Arban was instructor of cornet and trumpet at the Paris Conservatoire. He is most famous for his variation set for trumpet entitled *The Carnival of Venice*, a virtuoso showcase piece exemplary of nineteenth-century technical display. He also took an interest in the newly constructed saxhorn, or saxophone, as this piece shows. As a set of variations, how does it compare with the Haydn symphony and Beethoven piano sonata movements included earlier in this anthology?

VAR. III: Più lento

77. Allegro non troppo from Sonata for Cello and Piano in E Minor, Op. 38 *(1862–65)*

JOHANNES BRAHMS
(1833–97)
❖

Both the cellist and the pianist should listen carefully to the left hand of the piano part in preparing this piece for performance. There are a number of pedal tones and prolonged bass downbeat pitches that ultimately form deep-level stepwise lines across long spans of the music. How will an aural awareness of these help with shaping the presentation of form in this work?

78. Prelude for Organ, Op. 122, No. 3, "O Welt, ich muß dich lassen" *(1896)*

JOHANNES BRAHMS
(1833–97)

❖

Brahms wrote the Op. 122 chorales near the end of his life; unsurprisingly, more than half of them deal with the subject of human mortality. Brahms's treatment of this subject, however, is not necessarily in line with religious orthodoxy. In a letter to the critic Herzogenberg, who had recently maligned Brahms' work, he wrote, "I shall shortly be sending you some little things which you can attack for their 'un-Christian thinking' in your new journal." Note that Brahms didn't indicate tempi for any of the Op. 122 chorales; they must be determined by musical and textual clues alone. What tempo seems fitting for No. 3 here, and why?

79. Allegro appassionato from Sonata for Viola (or Clarinet) and Piano in E♭ Major, Op. 120, No. 2 *(1894)*

JOHANNES BRAHMS
(1833–97)
❖

Brahms's music is well known for its intricate metric play. In this movement, listen for examples of hemiola. Do they tend to occur anywhere in particular within phrases or formal sections? Are they created by contour, motive, harmony, or a combination of these? With what other metric and/or rhythmic processes do the examples of hemiola interact? And how can the exploitation of these metric and rhythmic processes come out in performance or analytic understanding?

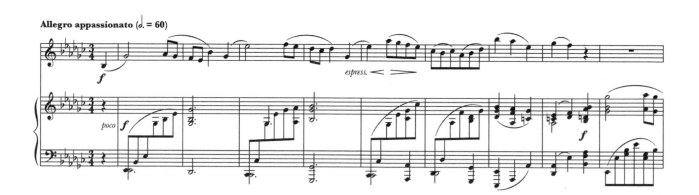

80. Two Rhapsodies for Piano, Op. 79
(1879)

JOHANNES BRAHMS
(1833–97)

❖

These are two separate works in distantly related keys, yet Brahms published them under the same opus number. This doesn't necessarily imply a musical connection between the two works, but scholars such as Rudolph Reti believe that the thematic materials in the two rhapsodies are related. What do you think? Compare the main melodic materials in the two rhapsodies. Are there underlying similarities?

NO. 1 IN B MINOR

NO. 2 IN G MINOR

81. Intermezzo for Piano in A Major, Op. 118, No. 2 *(1893)*

JOHANNES BRAHMS
(1833–97)

❖

Many musicians consider this work to be, in a word, a masterpiece. It displays a finely honed contrapuntal craft while simultaneously pouring out fluid melodies within limpid textures. Perhaps most importantly, the compositional technique is barely noticeable, its facility serving the larger goal of deep expression. Pay special attention to the opening six notes of the melody. Where and when do they return? Would you hear them if you weren't specifically listening for them? How might knowledge of this motive affect the pianist's realization of the texture? Also, consider the repeated section; given that there are really two melodies in it, the repeat allows the performer to voice the music differently each time it is played to make each of these tunes audible in turn.

82. Cavatine for Trombone and Piano, Op. 144 *(1915)*

CAMILLE SAINT-SAËNS
(1835–1921)

❖

In simple diatonic contexts, most students of harmony come to be familiarized fairly early on with sonorities that are best explained as prolongational or contrapuntal, rather than functional or cadential, in nature. Common examples include passing and neighboring chords and sequences. In later Romantic-era music, a number of more complex chromatic examples abound. One in this Cavatine by Saint-Saëns occurs in mm. 51–69. Many analysts would describe this music as a chain of semitonal voice-leading moves. Does this make sense to you? How do you hear this passage functioning, in terms of both the local chord progressions and its more global placement in the form as a whole?

83. Allegretto from Sonata for Clarinet and Piano in E♭ Major, Op. 167 *(1921)*

CAMILLE SAINT-SAËNS

(1835–1921)

❖

As is often the case in ternary forms, the contrasting B section in this movement is not unlike a sonata development with regard to its tonal instability. Tonal areas include F, Ab, and Cb. Local-level harmonic resolutions are also interesting to examine, with a number of common-tone chords and unusual augmented-sixth sonorities present. Does noting such things make any difference to the performance of this work? If so, how?

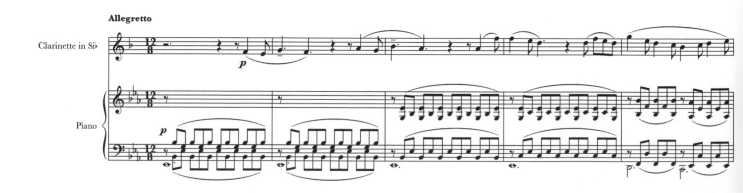

84. Morceau Symphonique for Trombone and Piano, Op. 88
(1898)

ALEXANDRE GUILMANT

(1837–1911)

❖

Rich chromatic harmonies pepper the surface of this music, particularly the Andante sostenuto. Find one that is particularly difficult to explain and challenge your classmates (or your instructor!) to make structural and musical sense of it.

85. "Septembre, La Chasse" from *Les Saisons*, Op. 37♭ *(1876)*

PYOTR TCHAIKOVSKY
(1840–93)

❖

As we might expect, this work titled "La Chasse" ("The Hunt") evokes the sounds of hunting horns. What figures specifically create this aural imagery? How are they woven into the structure of a quintessentially Romantic piano piece? Should the horn sounds be performed in a certain way to bring them out of the texture, or are they best integrated into a larger sound mass?

86. Selections from *Swan Lake* (1876)

PYOTR TCHAIKOVSKY

(1840–93)

❖

After its premier, Tchaikovsky's *Swan Lake* was criticized for being too "symphonic." Listeners used to a string of musically unrelated set pieces were surprised to hear a ballet rich with recurring transformed themes (leitmotivs). In retrospect, Tchaikovsky's approach was as transformative for setting new standards of dramatic unity in ballet as was Wagner's approach to opera. In addition to marking thematic recurrence and transformation, note that Tchaikovsky's chromatic harmony often stymies typical Roman-numeral analysis. Are there better explanations for the function of some of these chords?

NO. 17, SORTIE DES INVITES ET VALSE, CONCLUSION

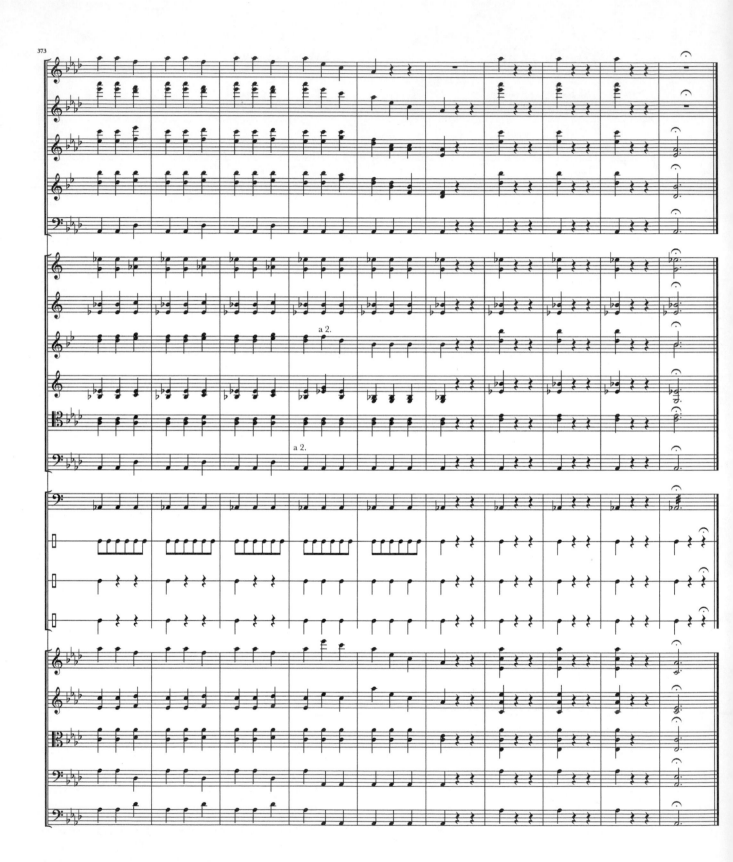

NO. 24, SCÈNE: ALLEGRO VIVO CONCLUSION (L'ISTESSO TEMPO)

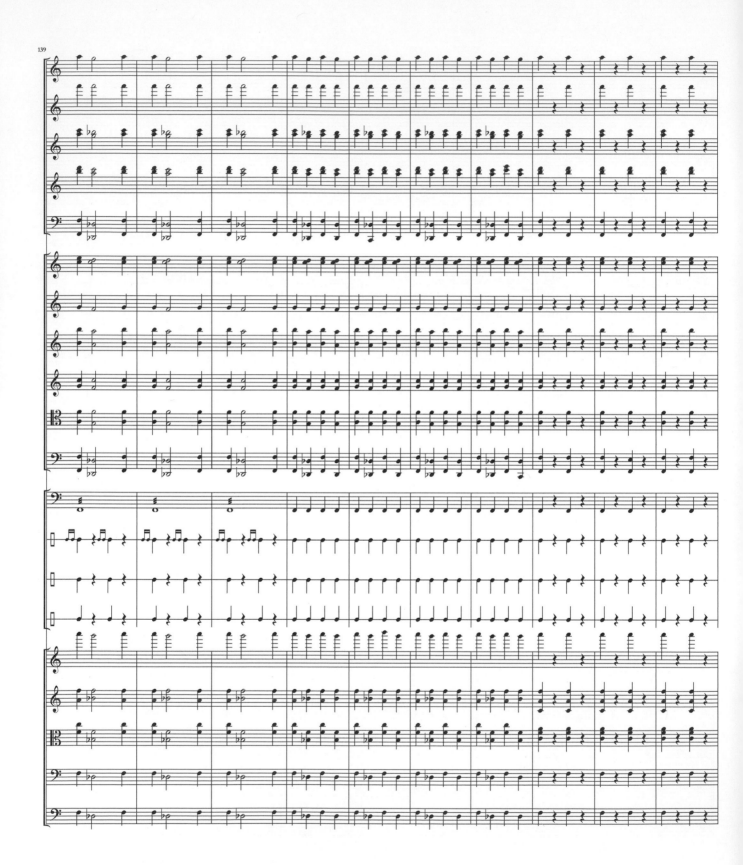

NO. 29, SCÈNE FINALE

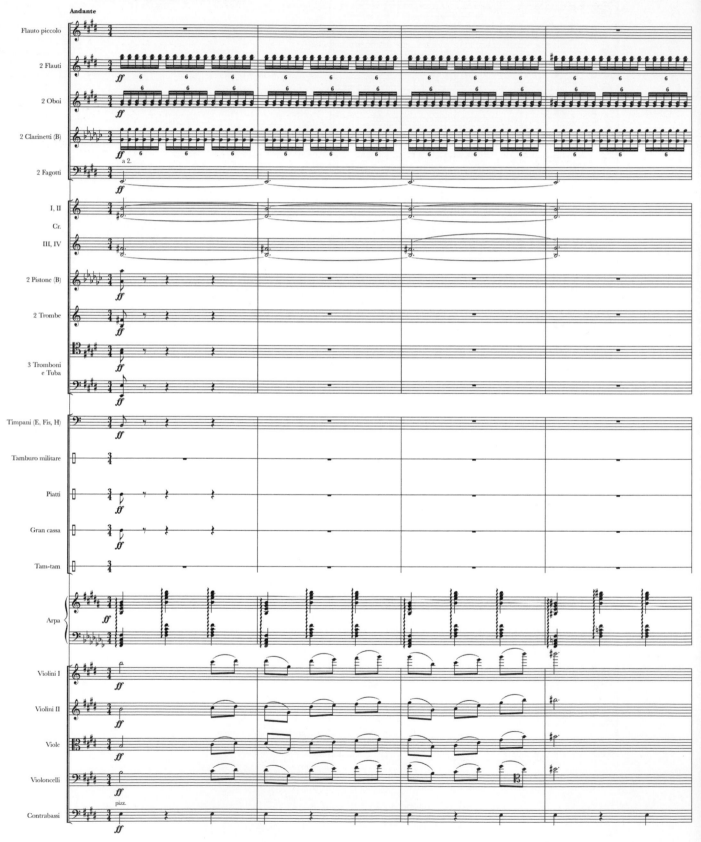

Alla breve. Moderato e maestoso

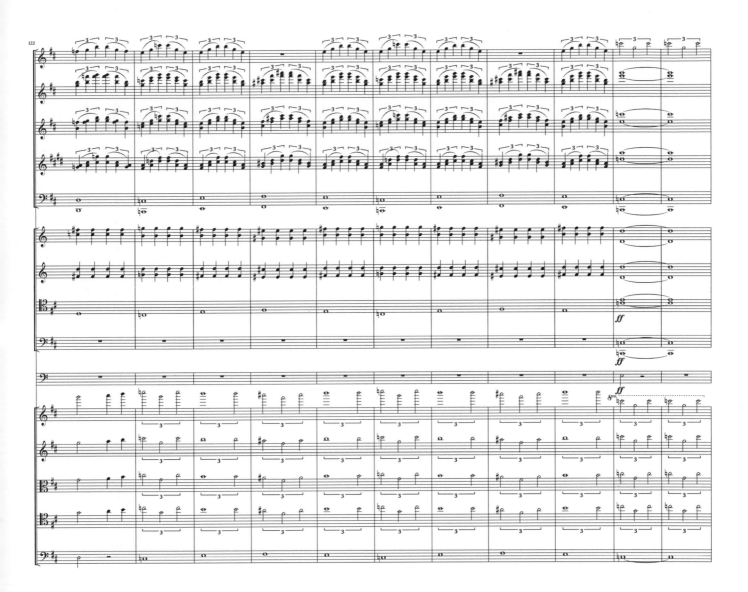

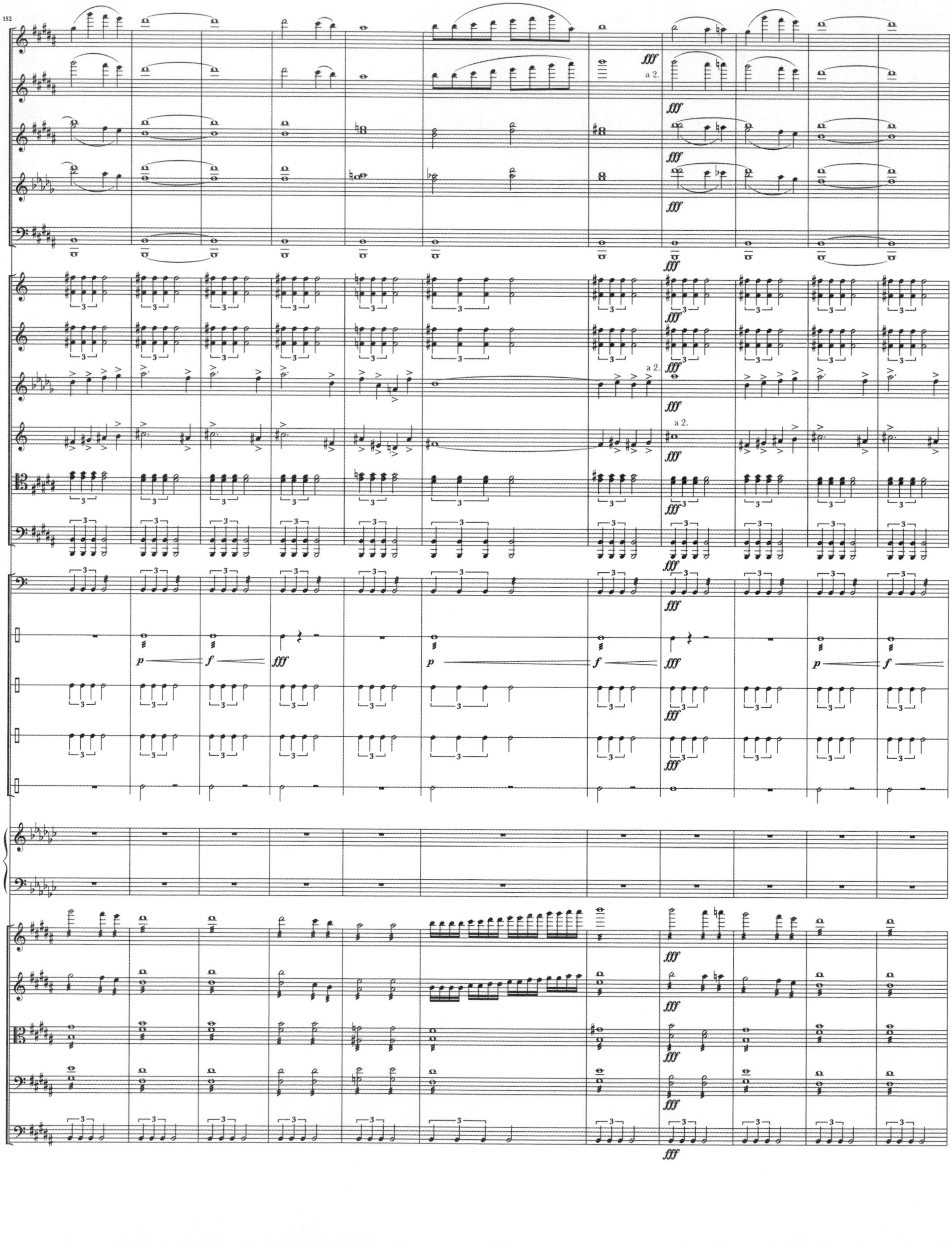
152
a 2.
a 2.
a 2.

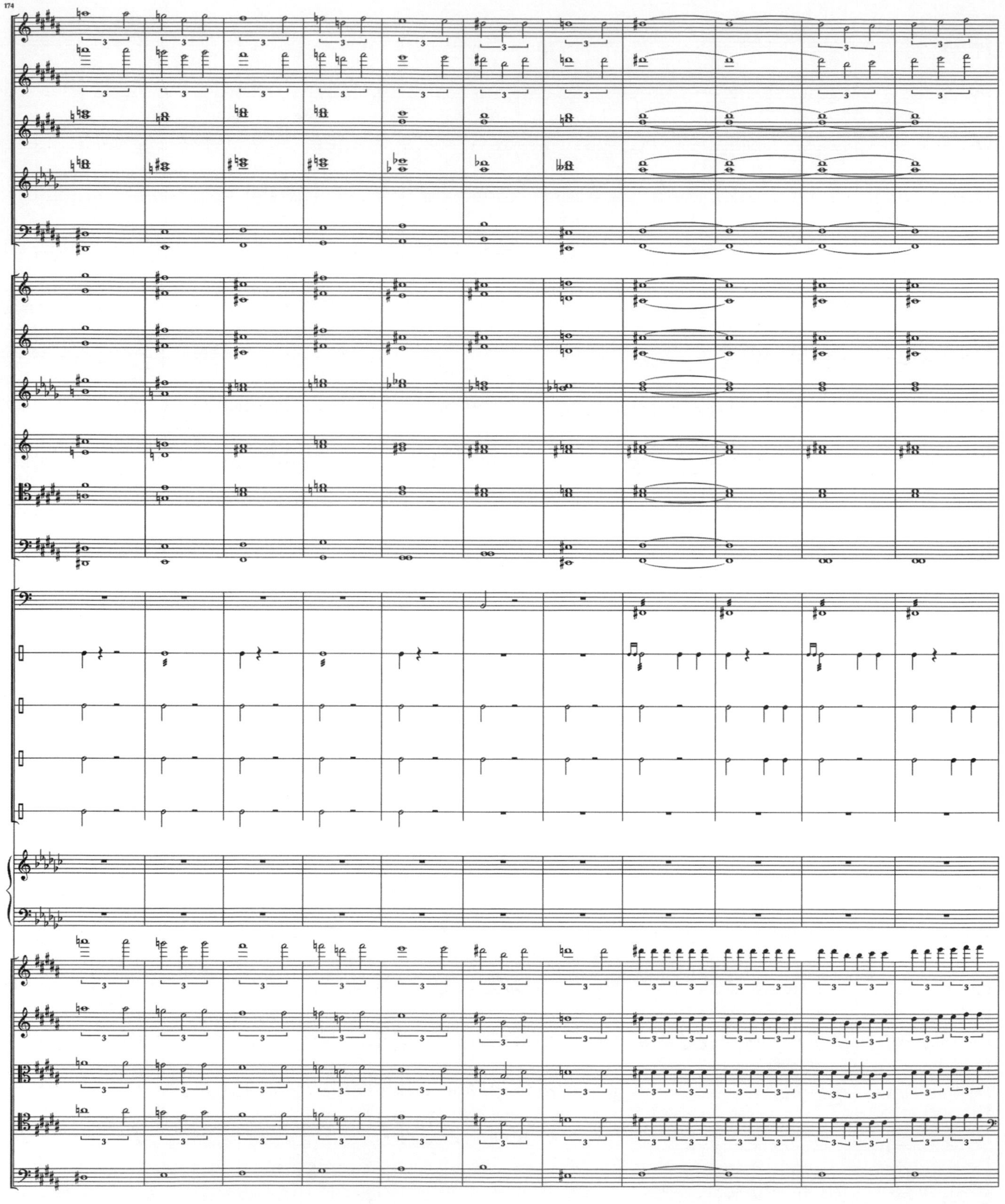
174

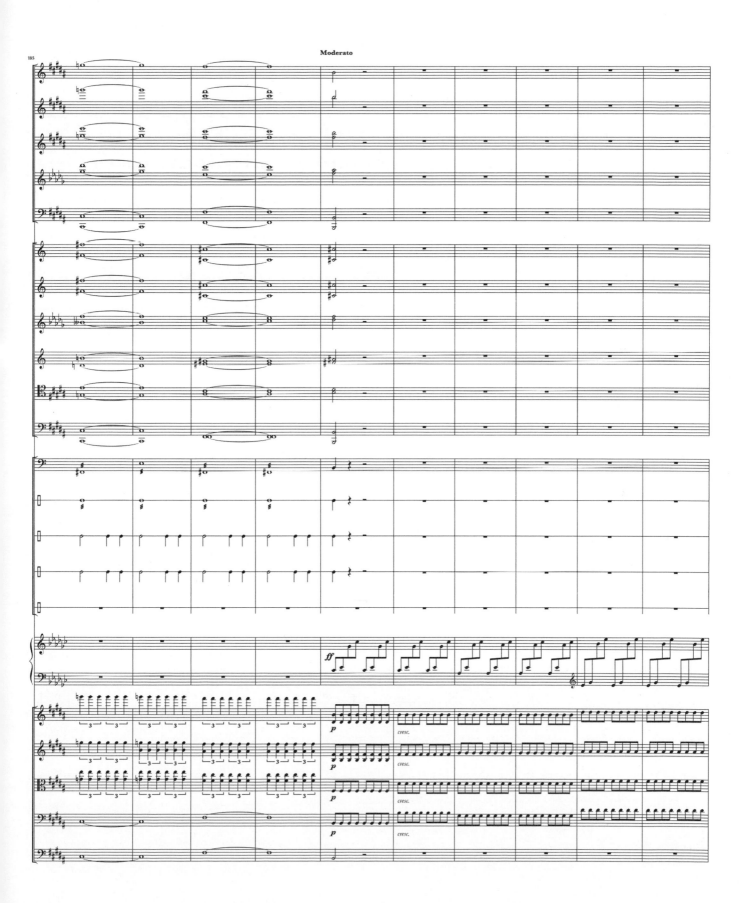

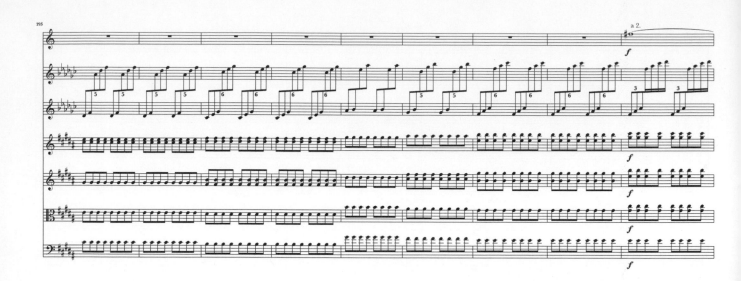

87. "Morning Prayer" from *Album for the Young (1878), arr. for marimba*

PYOTR TCHAIKOVSKY
(1840–93)
❖

Although this work is written for piano (here transcribed for marimba), its texture unarguably evokes the four-part chorale. Does the composition obey all the guidelines for chorale writing? What about its form? Is it a single phrase? A period? Is there an introduction or a coda? A climax? In short, how should it be shaped, as one musical gesture or a succession of them?

88. Slavonic Dance in F Major for Two Pianos, Op. 46, No. 4 *(1878)*

ANTONIN DVǑRÁK
(1841–1904)

❖

Because so much of Dvořák's music relies on modal folk idioms, it can have an uneasy relationship with the analytic tools developed for functionally monotonal music. Are there places where traditional Roman-numeral and figured-bass analysis seem to fall short in explaining the harmonic structure? Where? And how might we better explain these moments?

SECONDO

Tempo di minuetto

PRIMO

Tempo di minuetto

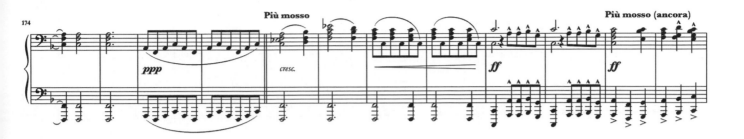

89. Two Piano Pieces

EDVARD GRIEG
(1843–1907)
❖

Both "Wedding Day at Troldhaugen" and "Little Troll" contain some amazing passages of chromaticism. Pay special attention to mm. 45–49 in "Wedding Day at Troldhaugen" and 21–37 in "Little Troll." Both effect chromatic modulations, but explaining the harmonies within these passages can be difficult. Is it better to think of them as conglomerations of chromatic lines rather than vertical harmonies? In either case, how does one shape these passages in performance?

Note that these works have been arranged for orchestra.

"WEDDING DAY AT TROLDHAUGEN" OP. 65, NO. 6 (1896)

"LITTLE TROLL" OP. 71, NO. 3 (1901)

90. Morceau de Lecture (Concours) for Flute and Piano
(1898)

GABRIEL FAURÉ
(1845–1924)
❖

Ask any professor at an institution of higher education about the balance among teaching, research, and service and you may get an earful! The demands on musicians today (and not just those affiliated with the academy) often include much more than performing or doing research, including teaching and administration. Gabriel Fauré was a model for this combination of labors; he was not only a composer but also taught composition, counterpoint, and fugue, and eventually he became the director of the Paris Conservatoire. Upon achieving this post, Fauré strove to break the unhealthy habit of using virtuosic test pieces to measure the abilities of instrumentalists studying at the Conservatoire. He favored instead test music that showcased phrasing, style, and rhythm. How do you think this work exhibits the new values Fauré hoped to instill in conservatory training?

91. "In dem Schatten meiner Locken" *(1889)*

HUGO WOLF
(1860–1903)
❖

As you listen to this lighthearted song, consider the nature of tonality and the relationship it might bear to the vagaries of the text (by Paul Heyse after an anonymous folk text). Is there only one tonic? If not, are all the key areas hierarchically equal? Do the changes of key reflect the text?

In the shadow of my hair
my sweetheart sleeps.
Shall I wake him? Ah, no!

Carefully I comb my tangled
locks early each day;
Yet all for naught is my effort,
for the wind messes them again.
The shadows of my hair, the whispering wind,
have lulled my sweetheart to sleep.
Shall I wake him? Ach, no!

I must listen to him complain
that he pines for me so long,
that life is given and taken from him
by my brown cheek,
And he calls me a snake;
Yet he fell asleep by me.
Shall I wake him? Ach, no!

Leicht, zart, nicht schnell

molto riten.   *a tempo*

In dem Schat-ten mei-ner Lo-cken schlief mir mein Ge-lieb - ter ein.   Weck ich ihn nun auf?

Ach nein!   Sorg lich strählt ich mei-ne krau-sen Lo-cken täg-lich in der

Frü - he,   doch um-sonst   ist mei-ne Mü - he, weil die Win - de sie zer-sau - sen.

poco rit.   *a tempo*

Lo-cken - schat-ten, Win-des - sau - sen schlä-fer-ten den Lieb - sten ein.   Weck ich ihn nun auf?

92. Andante moderato from Symphony No. 6 in A Minor *(1903–04)*

GUSTAV MAHLER
(1860–1911)
❖

Darcy (2001) believes this movement is difficult to understand in terms of common formal patterns taught in music courses: sonata, binary, ternary, rondo, and so forth. Rather, he argues that the Andante moderato comprises four "rotations" of material that complete a process he (and other scholars) calls "teleological genesis"—a sense that each rotation is building up toward an eventual revelatory or climactic goal. This process is interrupted by two "fantasy projections" that stand somewhat outside the narrative arc of the movement. Do you hear the movement this way? What implications might such a hearing have upon performance decisions in the work?

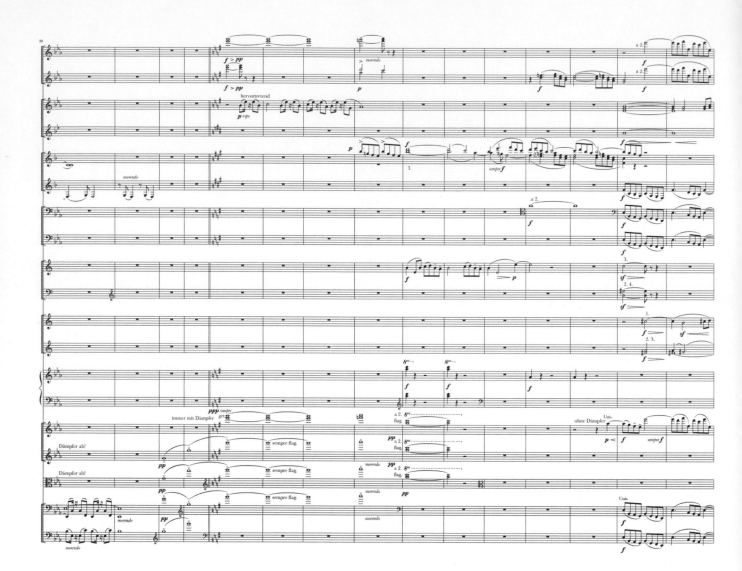

93. Moderato from Brass Quintet No. 1 in B♭ Minor
(c. 1890)

VICTOR EWALD
(1860–1935)

❖

Victor Ewald, a turn-of-the-century Russian composer, is little known outside of the brass community, where he is celebrated for penning the first music for what is now the standard brass quintet ensemble of two trumpets, horn, trombone, and tuba. Ewald's four quartets are all technically and musically challenging. The first one he wrote, now numbered as the fourth, was deemed too difficult to play on brass instruments and became a piece for strings instead. Does Ewald's writing in the present work strike you as idiomatic to brass instruments, or do traces of his predilection for string instruments remain?

Score in C

94. *Syrinx*
(1913)

CLAUDE DEBUSSY
(1862–1918)
❖

Single-line works appearing earlier in this anthology, like those by Telemann and Bach, often incorporate an implied sense of harmony, either through chordal arpeggiation or through evocation of common melodic or harmonic patterns. But what of this work? Does the flute line imply anything other than melody? If so, does a sense of tonality or of harmonic function seem present in this music? Why or why not? Must a performer approach this work gesturally, or are there larger organizational principles at work?

«Tais-toi, contiens ta joie, écoute.»

95. Two Preludes

CLAUDE DEBUSSY
(1867–1918)
❖

A. "Danseuses de Delph" (1910)

Claude Debussy wrote many of his piano preludes after being inspired by certain images or experiences. "Danseuses de Delph" ("Delphic Dancers"), for instance, came about after the composer was struck by the beauty of ancient artwork, specifically, sculpted figures atop a Greek pillar. Delphi, the city from which the dancers come, is both a modern town in Greece and an archaeological site. In ancient times it was home to the most important oracle in the Mediterranean world and also hosted pan-Hellenic games, precursors of the Olympiad. Do you think Debussy's music exhibits a dance form or rather evokes the experience of *watching* dancers, perhaps dancers who, like the oracle, had fallen into a mystical trance? Why?

Listen also for Debussy's extended tonal techniques in this work. How do augmented triads, planing (parallel motion through pitch space of the same sonority type, e.g., dominant seventh chords), and real transposition affect the senses of harmonic function, form, and overall tonality?

B. "Feux d'artifice" (1913)

"Feux d'artifice" ("Fireworks") is another work in which extended tonal techniques contribute to the form, expressive content, and sense of tonality. Listen especially for the pervasive transformations of the opening major-third motive. Can you also hear a quotation from *La Marseillaise*?[10]

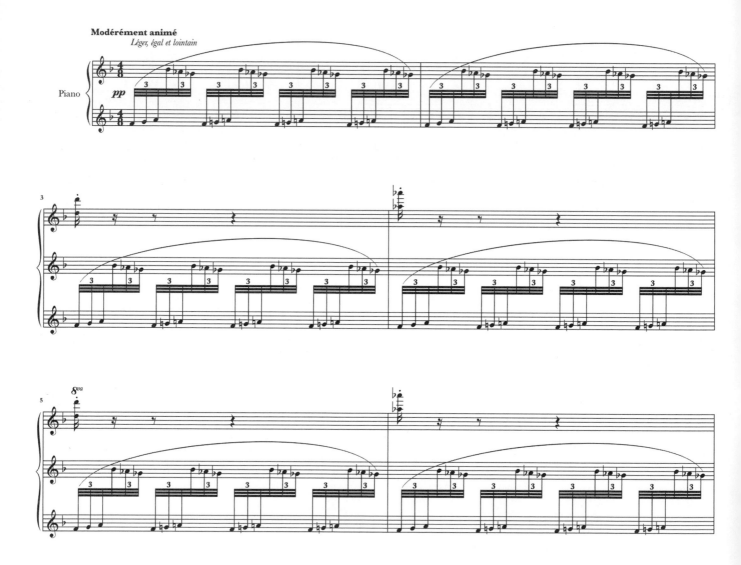

[10]See Lewin (1993) for a thoroughgoing motivic, formal, and transformational analysis that takes nationalism into account.

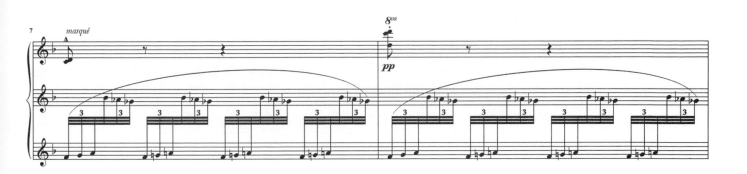

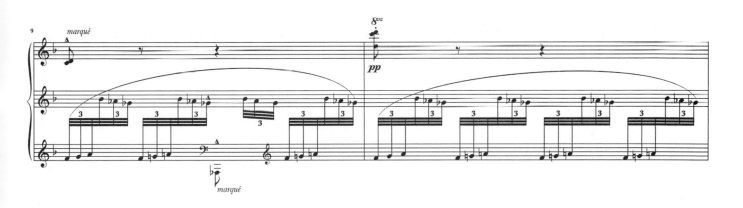

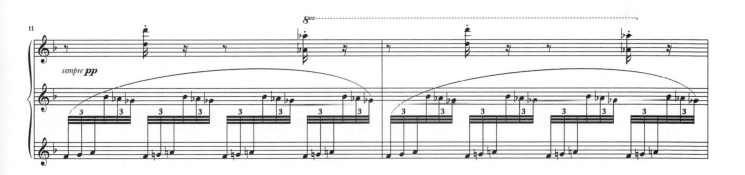

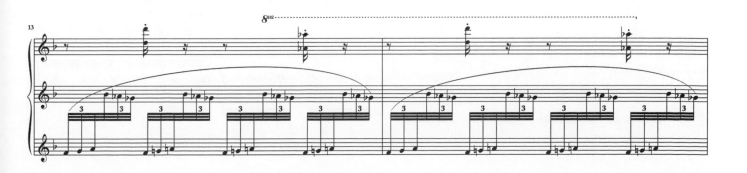

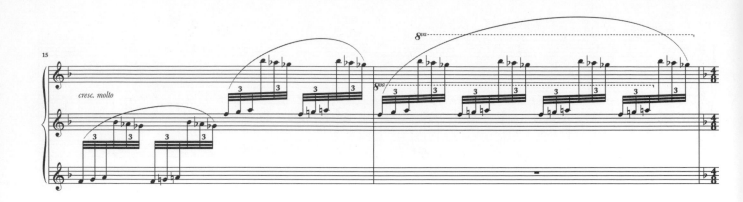

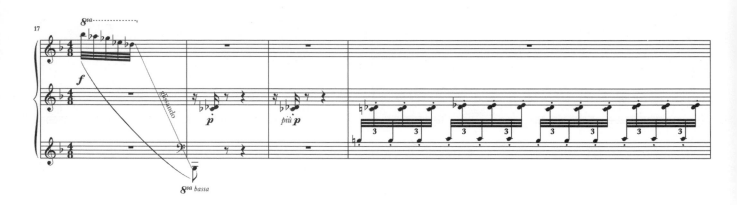

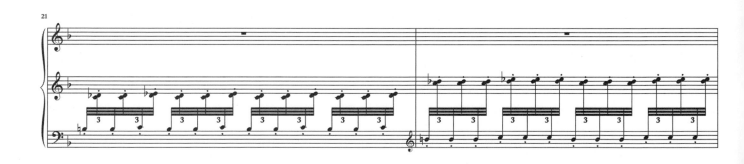

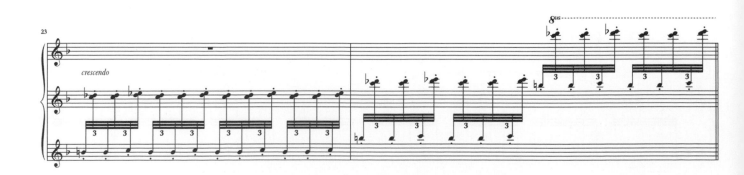

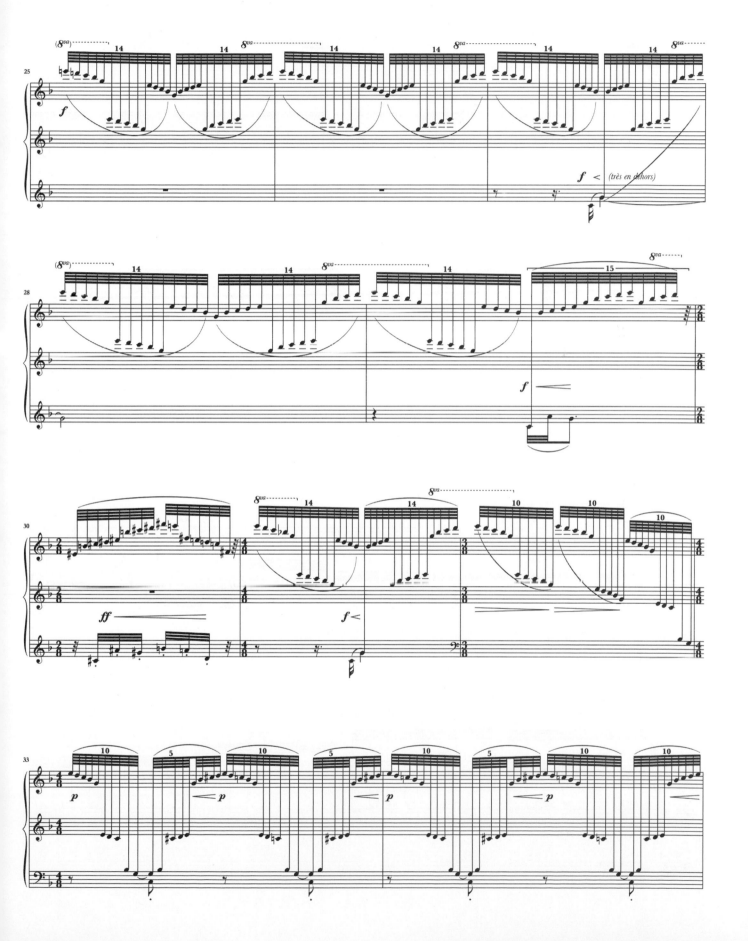

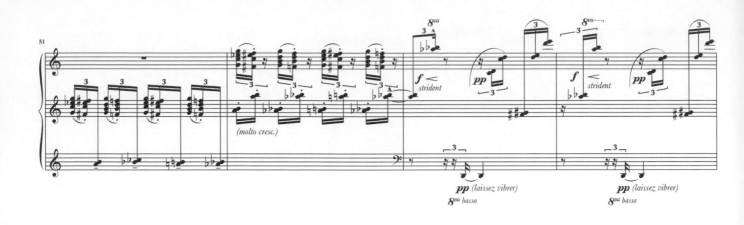

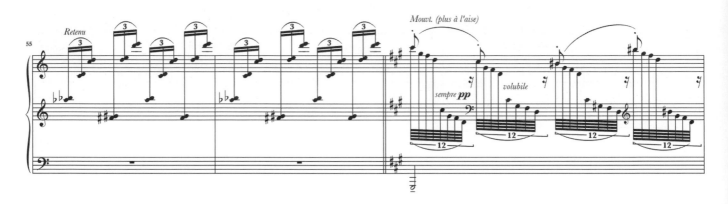

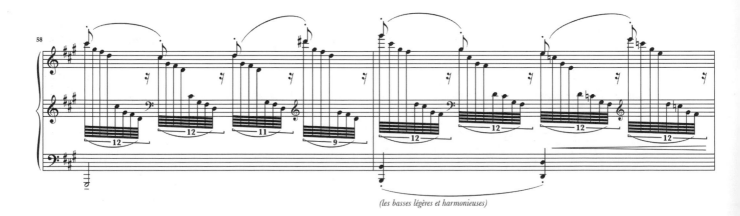

Doux et harmonieux (Molto Rubato)

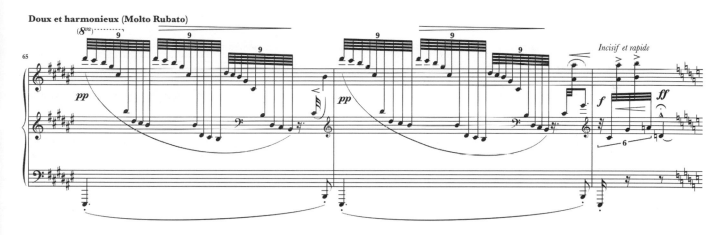

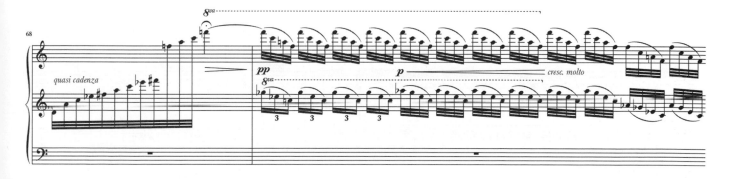

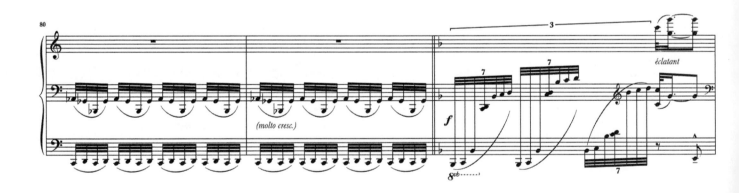

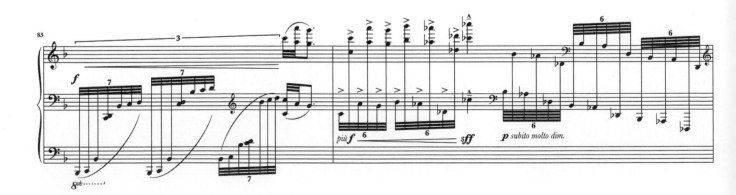

96. Two Songs from Op. 27
(1894)

RICHARD STRAUSS
(1864–1949)

❖

Strauss composed his Op. 27 songs in the six months before his marriage to soprano Pauline de Ahna. They are grouped together under the same opus number but do not make up a true cycle like Schubert's *Die schöne Müllerin* or Schumann's *Dichterliebe*. The first song, "Ruhe, meine Seele," presents profound interpretive challenges. The texture and ambiguous tonality of the first thirteen bars are suggestive of recitative. From m. 14 on, the song adopts a four-bar hypermetric regularity, but the sense of form and tonal center remain anything but obvious. Marvin and Rolf (1990) point to the four-note voice leading paradigm G–F#–F–E in the piano as a point of cohesion that can be brought out in performance. Stein and Spillman (1996, 196–97) argue that the song comprises two strophes from the pianist's point of view, but its form is more complicated from the singer's point of view, raising the question of two competing musical personas in performance. Is there anything similar going on in "Morgen!"?

NO. 1 "RUHE, MEINE SEELE!"

And tomorrow the sun will shine again,
and on the path I will take,
it will unite us again, we happy ones,
upon this sun-breathing earth. . . .

And to the shore, the wide shore with blue waves,
we will descend quietly and slowly;
we will look mutely into each other's eyes
and the silence of happiness will settle upon us.

Translation: Emily Ezust

Herz und Hirn in Not Ru - he, ru - he mei-ne See - le, und ver - giss, und ver-

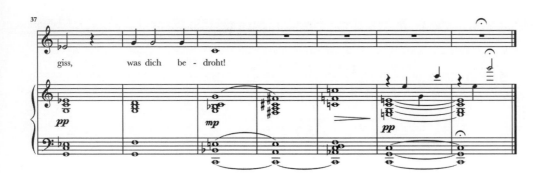

giss, was dich be - droht!

NO. 4 "MORGEN!"

Not a breeze is stirring lightly,
the wood lies slumbering gently;
through the dark cover of leaves
steals bright sunshine.

Rest, rest, my soul,
your storms have gone wild,
have raged and trembled
like the surf when it breaks.

These times are powerful,
bringing torment to heart and mind;
rest, rest, my soul,
and forget what is threatening you!

Translation: Emily Ezust

sehr ruhig

Und mor-gen wird die Son-ne wie - der schei - nen und auf dem We - ge, den ich ge - hen wer - de, wird

uns, die Glück - li -chen, sie wie - der ei - - nen in-mit-ten die-ser son - nen at - men-den Er - de...

und zu dem Strand, dem wei - ten, wo-gen-blau - en, wer-den wir still und lang-sam nie-der-stei-gen,

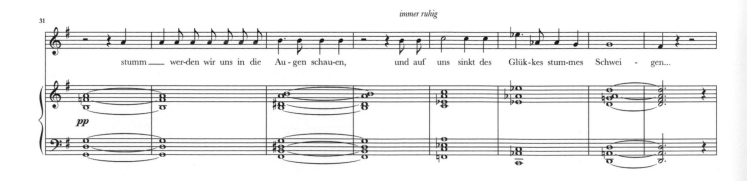

immer ruhig

stumm ___ wer-den wir uns in die Au - gen schau-en, und auf uns sinkt des Glük-kes stum-mes Schwei - gen...

97. "Ah, Love, but a Day!"
Op. 44, No. 2
(1900)

AMY CHENEY BEACH
(1867–1944)
❖

Virtually all texted music relies in some measure on the form of its text for its overall shape. Strophic poetic forms (that is, those based on strophes of text—for instance, quatrains) can result in strophic musical forms in which each strophe of text is sung to the same music. At times composers will alter texts, repeating or omitting lines to achieve a more satisfying musical form or expression. How do you hear the form of the text and the music in this work? Given that the text (by the poet Robert Browning) pre-dated Beach's setting, does its form seem to have influenced the form of the music, either in the small details or in the larger shape? If so, how?

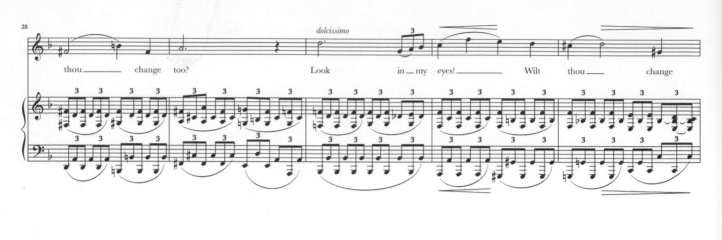

98. Two Preludes

ALEXANDER SCRIABIN
(1871/72–1915)

❖

PRELUDE IN A MINOR, OP. 11, NO. 2 (1888)

Scriabin's music is often cited as a bridge between chromatic, functional tonality and the other methods composers of the early twentieth century used to establish tonal coherence. Though at first hearing, this prelude may not sound tonal in the same as was, say, Mozart's music, it is surprising how useful traditional Roman numeral analysis can be in teasing apart the sense of underlying functional tonal progressions. Underneath the chromatic surface, what recognizable patterns can you find here that derive from earlier music?

PRELUDE IN G MINOR, OP. 27, NO. 1 (1900)

Though they are separated by only twelve years, Op. 11, No. 2 Op. 27, No. 1 have radically different approaches to tonality. How has Scriabin's compositional technique evolved in this later prelude, compared to the earlier one?

99. Vocalise, Op. 34, No. 14
(1912), arr. for tuba

SERGEI RACHMANINOV

(1873–1943)

❖

A vocalise is a vocal exercise without text. It is performed on a neutral syllable, like "ah" or "ooh." Although Rachmaninov's vocalise was written originally for solo voice, it has been arranged many times for instrumentalists, among them wind and brass players. Performing vocalises such as this one on wind instruments can be excellent training in mimicking the human voice and establishing a singing tone, ostensibly the goal of every single-line instrumentalist. How does Rachmaninov construct phrases in this work to accommodate the melodic-line performer's need to breathe?

100. Second Suite for Military Band in F Major
(1911)

GUSTAV HOLST
(1874–1934)

❖

Although its title implies that this work was written for performance by members of an armed service, in fact the term *military band* had come to mean something more like "concert band" or "community band" by the time Holst wrote his two suites. The origins of the wind ensemble in Western Europe arise from two eighteenth-century phenomena in Germany: the *Harmonie* or wind ensemble for an aristocratic court, and the true military ensemble, which started as little more than fifes, bugles, and drums. Note that the movements here pay tribute to both traditions; the "March" evokes a military procession, while the "Song Without Words" stems more from the tradition of art music. Regarding the latter, without words, are there structural elements to this piece that make it sound like a song?

MARCH

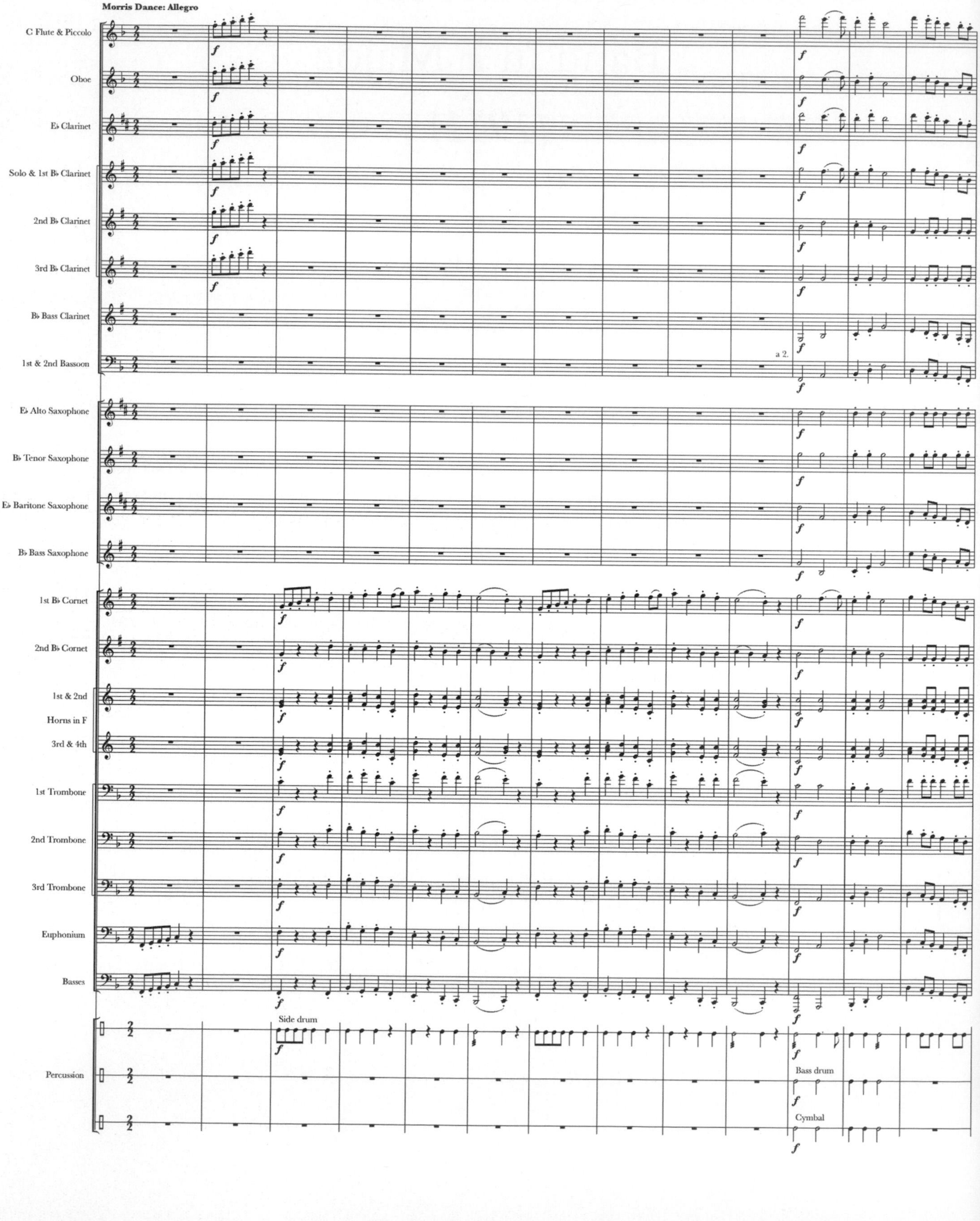
Morris Dance: Allegro
C Flute & Piccolo
Oboe
E♭ Clarinet
Solo & 1st B♭ Clarinet
2nd B♭ Clarinet
3rd B♭ Clarinet
B♭ Bass Clarinet
1st & 2nd Bassoon
a 2.
E♭ Alto Saxophone
B♭ Tenor Saxophone
E♭ Baritone Saxophone
B♭ Bass Saxophone
1st B♭ Cornet
2nd B♭ Cornet
1st & 2nd
Horns in F
3rd & 4th
1st Trombone
2nd Trombone
3rd Trombone
Euphonium
Basses
Side drum
Percussion
Bass drum
Cymbal

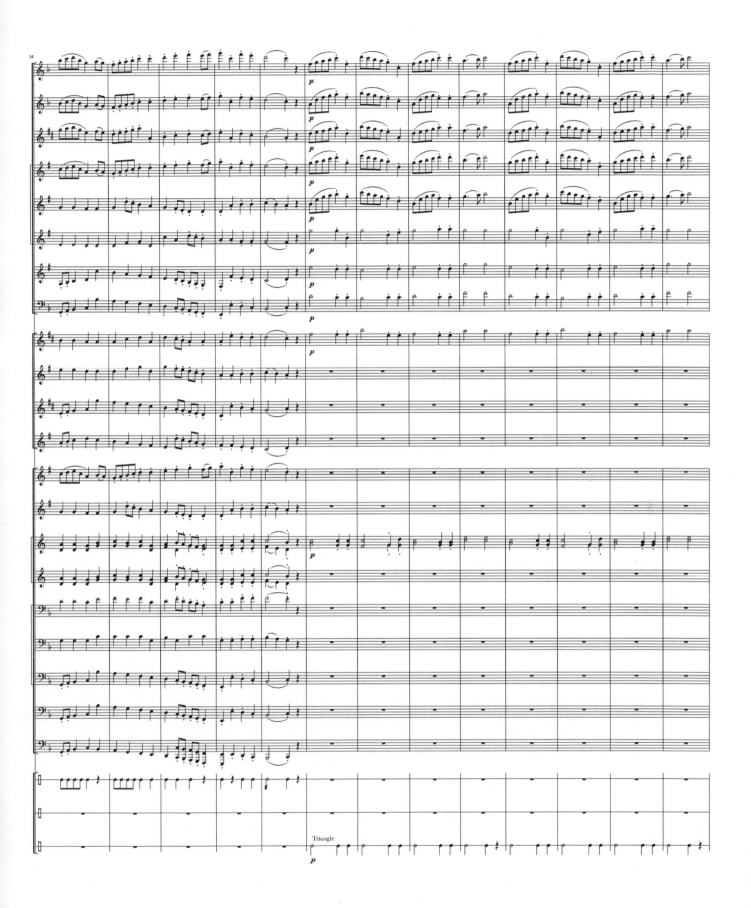

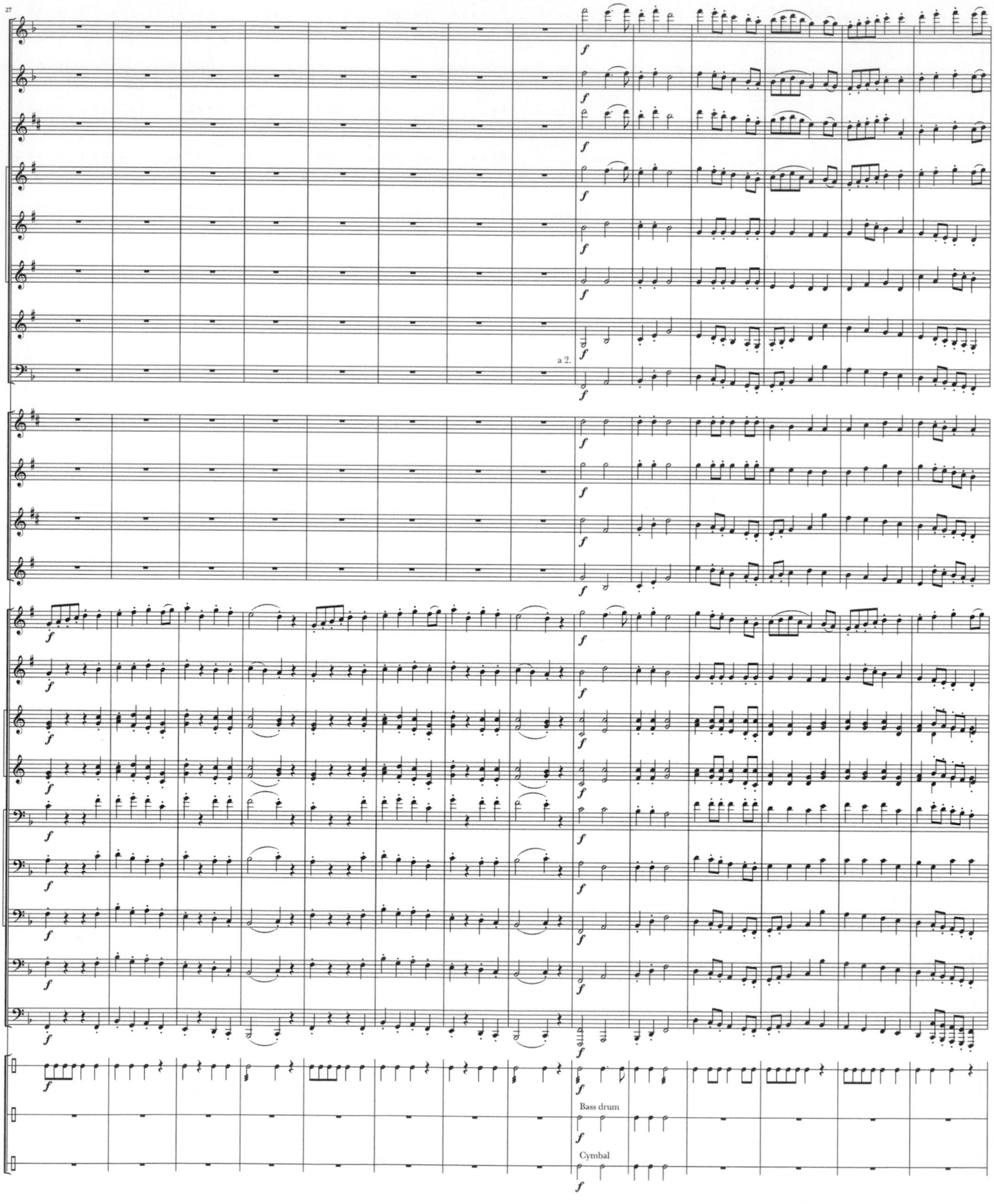
27
a 2.
Bass drum
Cymbal

Swansea Town

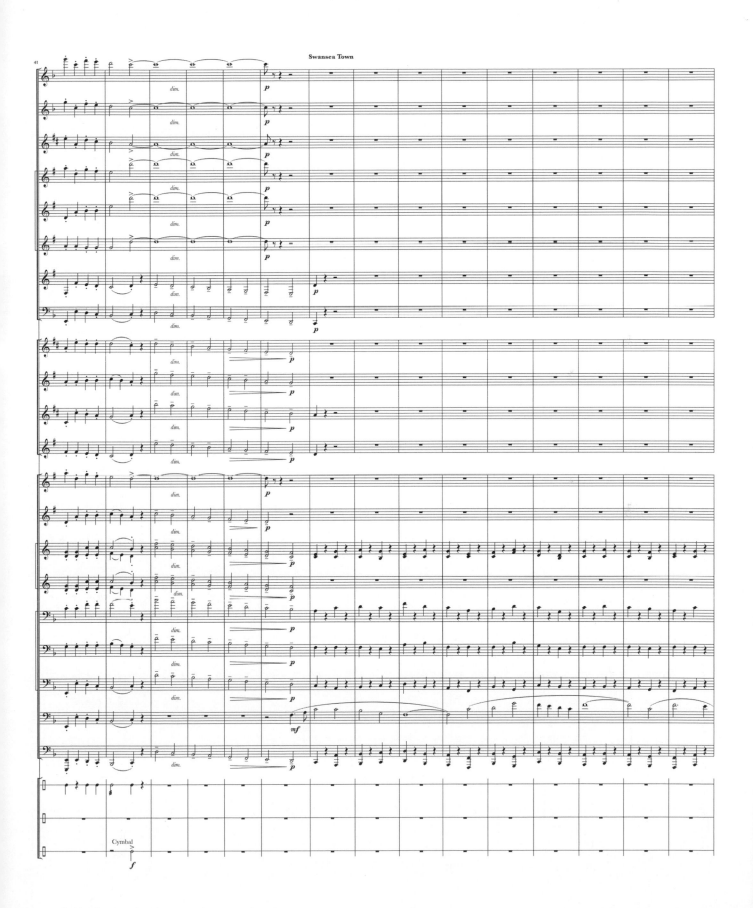

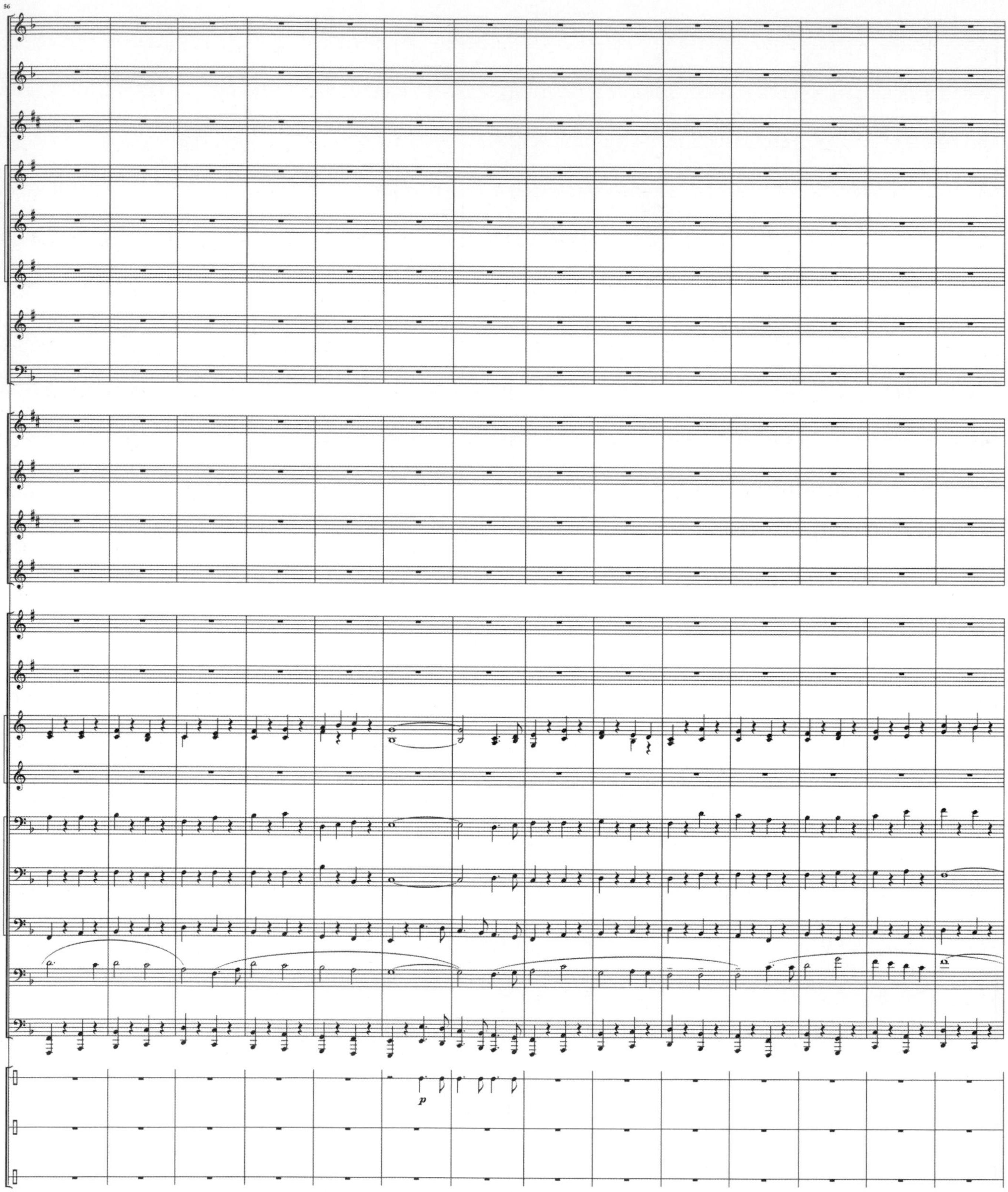
56
p

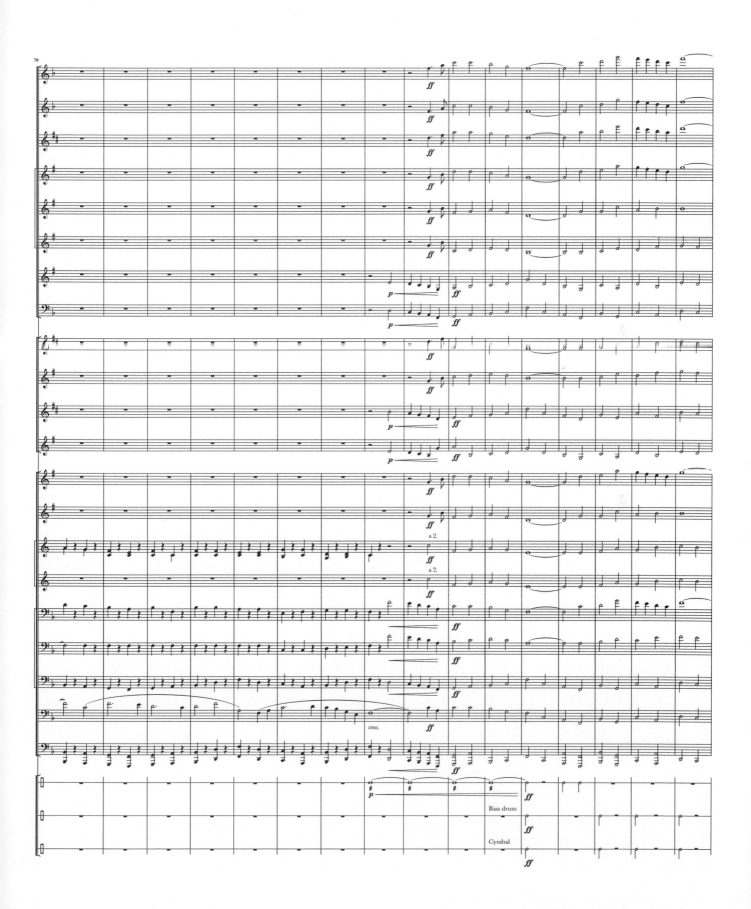

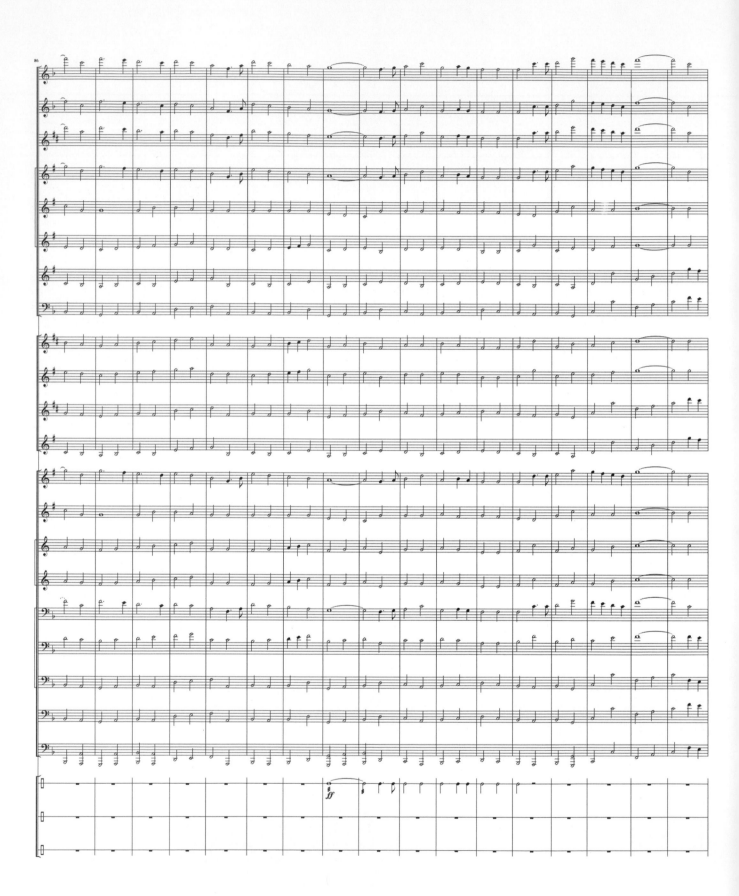

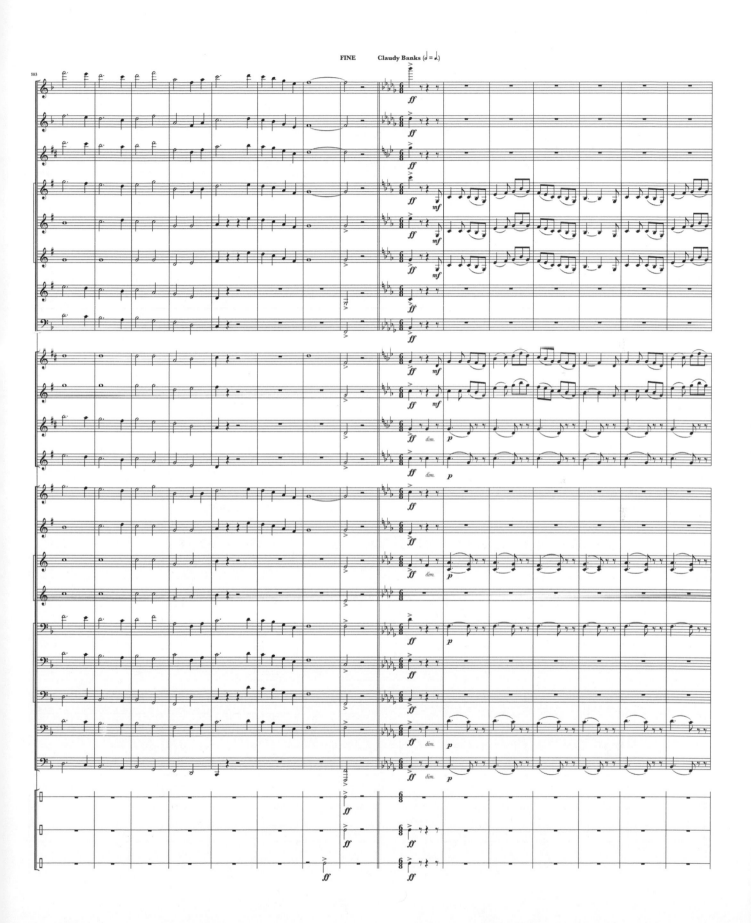

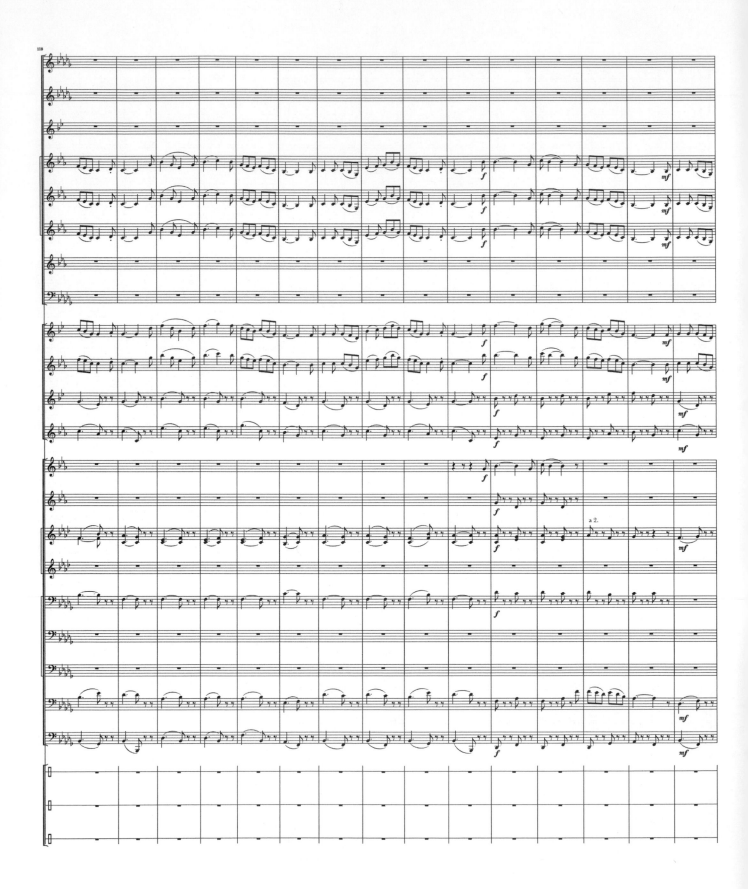

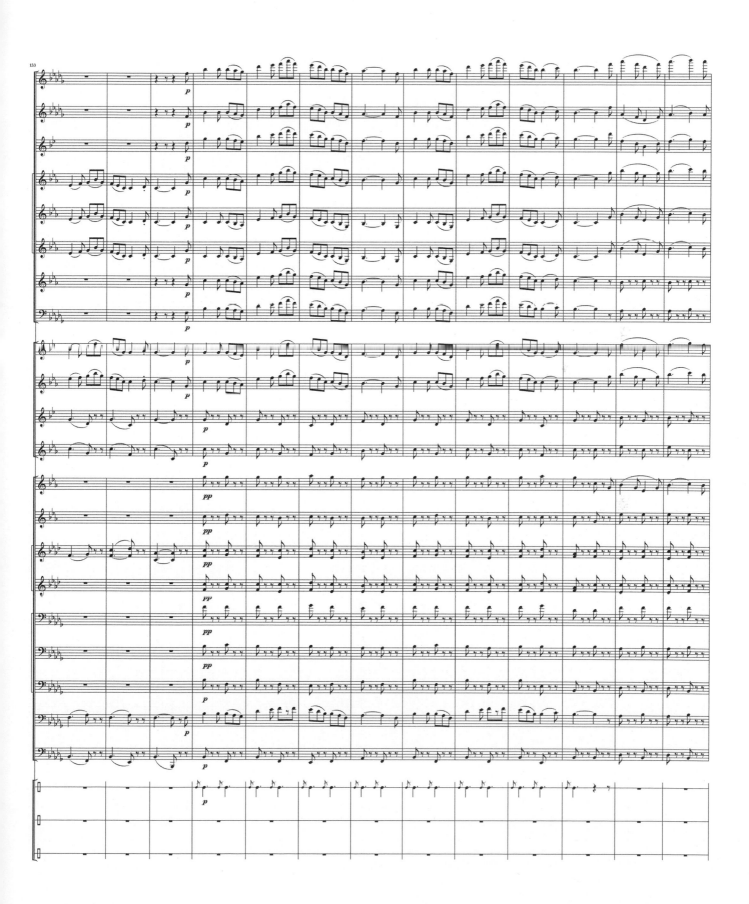

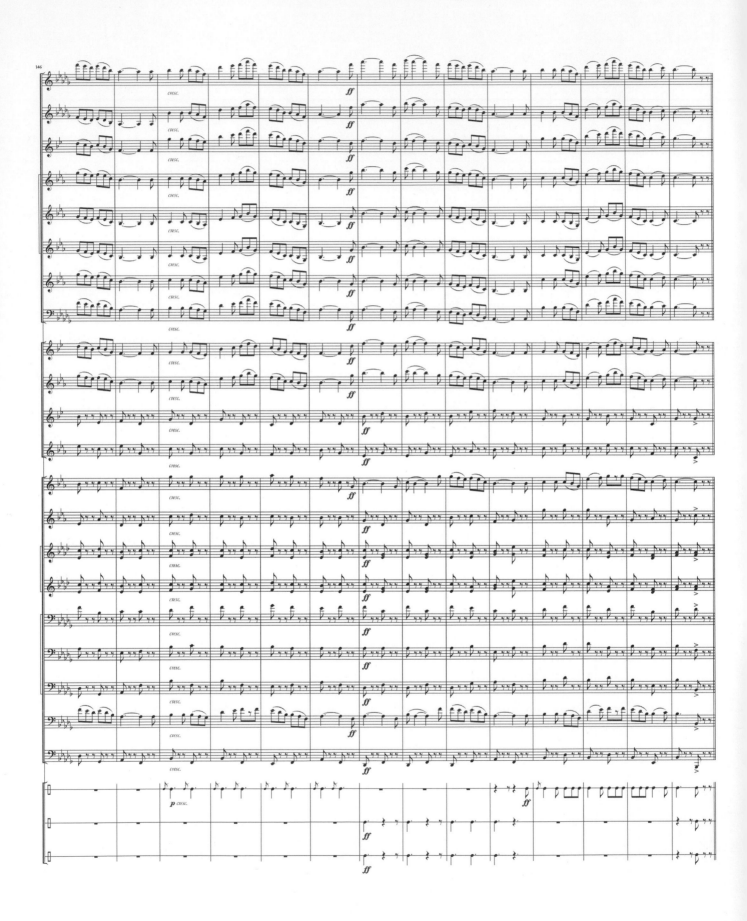

SONG WITHOUT WORDS

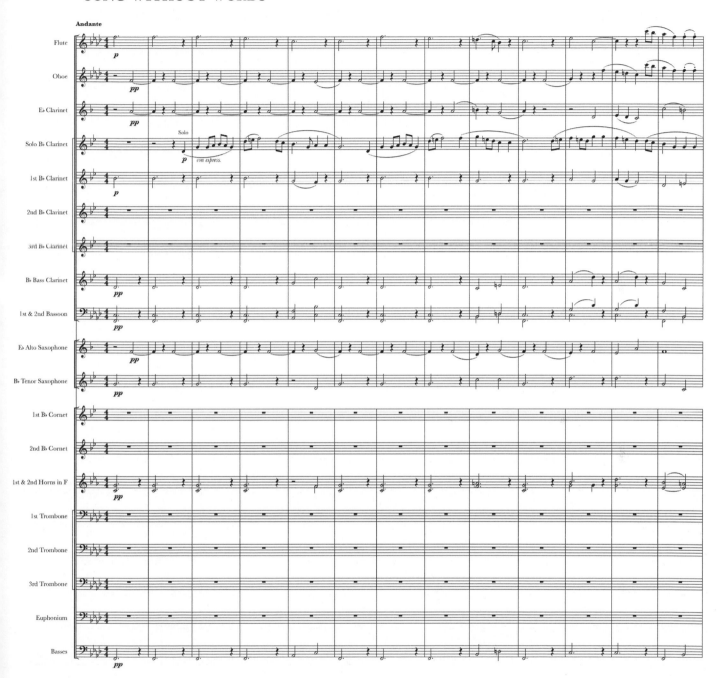

101. *Chanson Triste* for Double Bass and Piano, Op. 2 *(1949)*

SERGEI KOUSSEVITZKY

(1874–1951)

❖

Serge Koussevitzky is best remembered in the annals of North American music history as the conductor of the Boston Symphony Orchestra. He got his start in the music profession, however, as a virtuoso bassist. A champion of new music (particularly Russian music), Koussevitzky was a composer in his own right, with the bulk of his music, like this *Chanson Triste*, featuring the double bass. What is there about this music that makes it sound like a *chanson triste* (sad song)?

102. *Klavierstück*, Op. 11, No. 1
(1909)

ARNOLD SCHOENBERG
(1874–1951)
❖

It is difficult to exaggerate the historical importance of Schoenberg's Op. 11 piano pieces; they are arguably the composer's first "atonal" works. The chromaticism in No. 1 is obvious, but it is Schoenberg's use of motivic unity trumping tonal unity in providing artistic cohesion, rather than extreme chromaticism in the work, that scholars have focused on when explaining what technical means composers used to break with common-practice tonality.

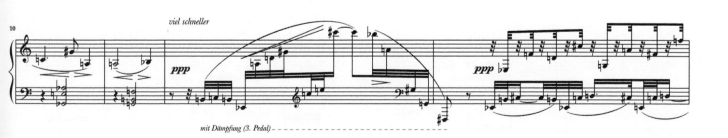

103. *Klavierstücke*, Op. 19, Nos. 2, 4, and 6 *(1923)*

ARNOLD SCHOENBERG
(1874–1951)

❖

These miniatures display a remarkable economy of means. Despite their brevity, though, they each manage to present at least one basic sonic idea and some form of contrast to it. Trichordal collections seem to be of particular importance. How?

NO. 2

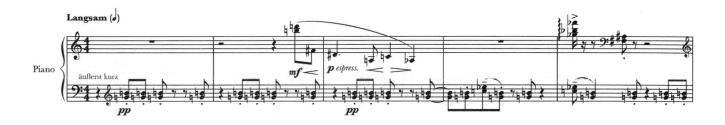

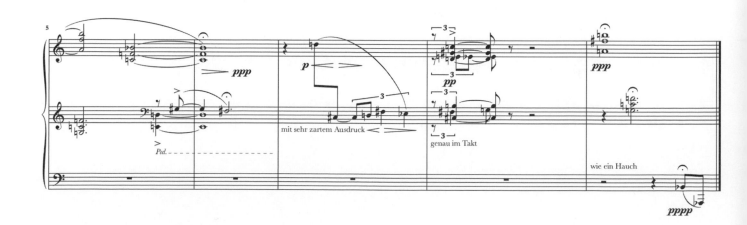

NO. 4

NO. 6

104. *Verbundenheit*, Op. 35, No. 6 *(1930)*

ARNOLD SCHOENBERG

(1874–1951)

If one knows the choral music of Anton Bruckner, it is hard not to hear Schoenberg's Op. 35 as an homage to his fellow Viennese predecessor. Of particular interest is how Schoenberg draws triadic sonorities from underlying twelve-tone compositional materials.

OBLIGATION

Thy birth with care is tended,   Blessings on thee!
A grave is dug for thee,   Rest in peace!
Thy wounds are nursed in the hospital   Quick recovery!
Quenched thy fires, thyself saved from drowning   Have no fear.
Thou, thy self, hast compassion for others   Help is near, thou art not alone!
Thou leavest not age to lie low   thou mayest fall so!
Thou bearest the load of the helpless   asking nought,
Though stayest the rush of the frightened horse   sparest thyself not,
Stoppest thieves, guardest they neighbor's welfare   undeterred, lendest thine succor.
Canst deny, that thou, too, dost here belong?   thou art not alone!

Translation: D. Millar Craig and Adolph Weiss

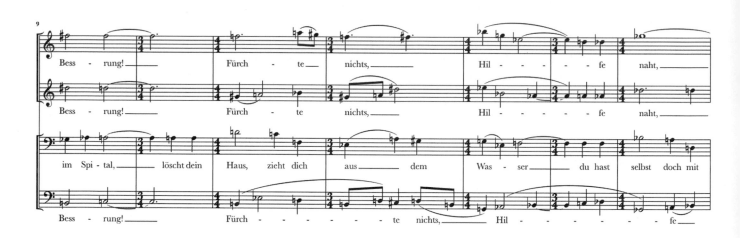

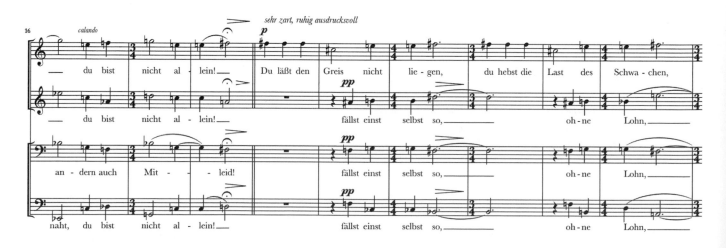

105. Mouvement de Menuet from *Sonatine* for Piano *(1903–05)*

MAURICE RAVEL
(1875–1937)
❖

Obviously, this work is inspired by the eighteenth-century triple-meter aristocratic dance. There are, however, formal, rhythmic, and tonal distinctions from the norms of the Classic-era minuet. Can you identify them?

106. Intermezzo for String Bass and Piano, Op. 9
(1908)

REINHOLD GLIÈRE
(1875–1956)
❖

In many works of Western art music, there are details that can be traced—like red threads in a tapestry—through the texture of the music. The use of B♭ in this A Major work stands as an example here. Where do linear and harmonic B♭'s occur, and how do they function? Does their recurrent presence suggest highlighting them in performance? If so, how?

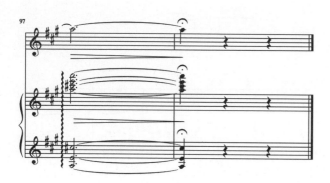

107. Two Selections from *Mikrokosmos* (1926, 1932–39)

BÉLA BARTÓK

(1881–1945)

❖

Mikrokosmos, Bartók's collection of short piano works, comprises more than 150 separate pieces. Their purpose is to train young musicians, and the works in the collection range from very simple to highly advanced. "From the Island of Bali" and "Diminished Fifths" fall into the simple category, at least in terms of the technique required to play them. The pitch collection Bartók uses—the octatonic scale—is not, however, one most beginning piano students trained in the West would be familiar with. How are subsets of the octatonic treated in these two works. What role does inversional symmetry have to play between the two hands?

"FROM THE ISLAND OF BALI"

"DIMINISHED FIFTHS"

108. Allegro from String Quartet No. 4 *(1928)*

BÉLA BARTÓK
(1881–1945)

❖

Some musicians argue that the first movement of Bartók's Fourth String Quartet is cast in sonata form. The first theme emerges from an imitative, polyphonic texture at the opening of the work. Eventually all four instruments play this motive in rhythmic unison, leading to a cadence. At this point a new, rocking texture begins. This new texture and the first, aggressive motive both return frequently throughout the movement, oftentimes sounding as if they are in conflict with one another.

Others would argue, however, that sonata form is predicated more on a *tonal* rather than a *thematic* contrast. Many composers wrote sonata forms that had only one theme. And others wrote sonata forms with three or more. What Classic- and early Romantic-era sonata forms shared was modulation in the exposition and an eventual return to the opening tonic key—a return that brought foreign-key themes into relation with the tonic during the recapitulation. Given this definition, it is hard to justify Bartók's string quartet movement as a *bona fide* sonata form. But perhaps the merits of calling it a sonata form—especially when making performance decisions—outweigh the problems. What do you think?

109. *Tema con variatione* from Octet *(1923)*

IGOR STRAVINSKY
(1882–1972)

❖

Though many variation forms contain a formal type for the theme, it is rare to find continuous, larger-scale formal processes across the entirety of a variation set. Even rarer is a composer choosing to blend the variation principle with another formal principle. This is, however, Stravinsky's strategy here; the recurring first variation creates a kind of rondo-form overlay atop the variation structure.

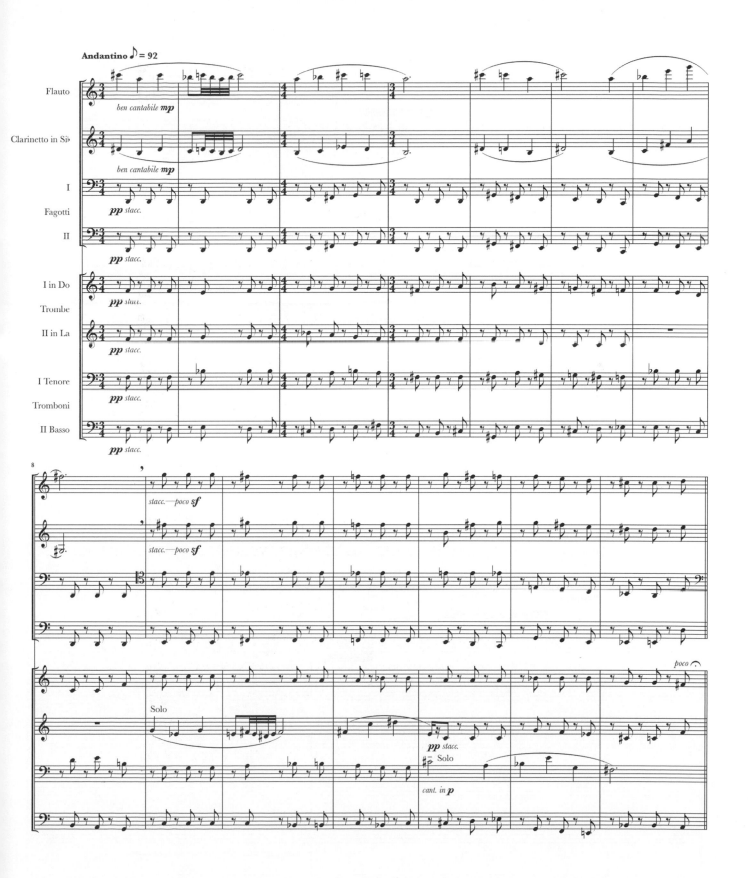

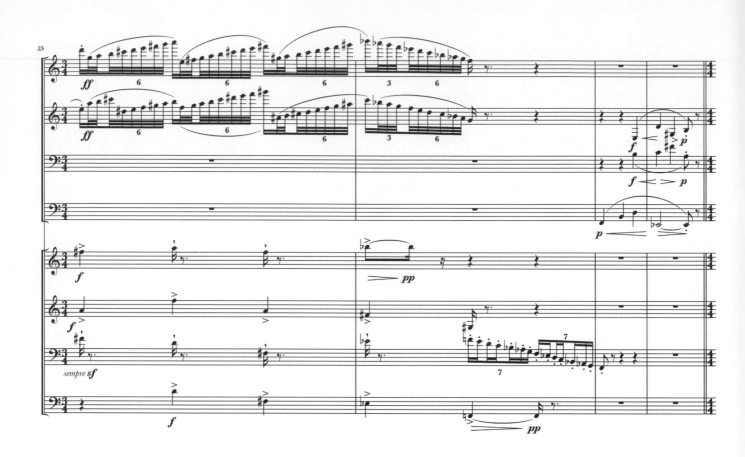

VAR. B ♩ = 120-126

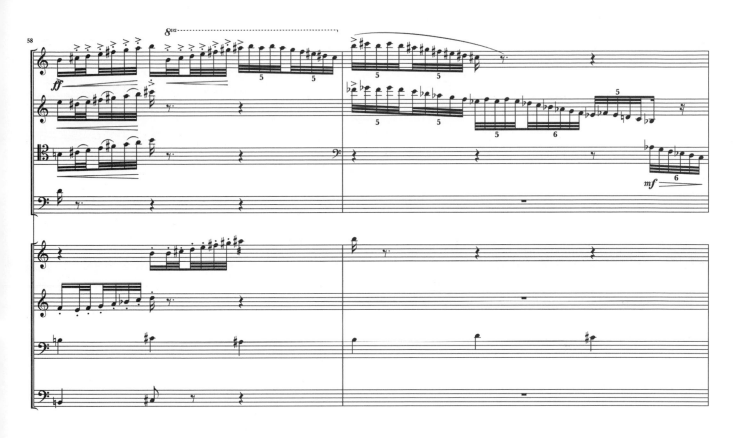

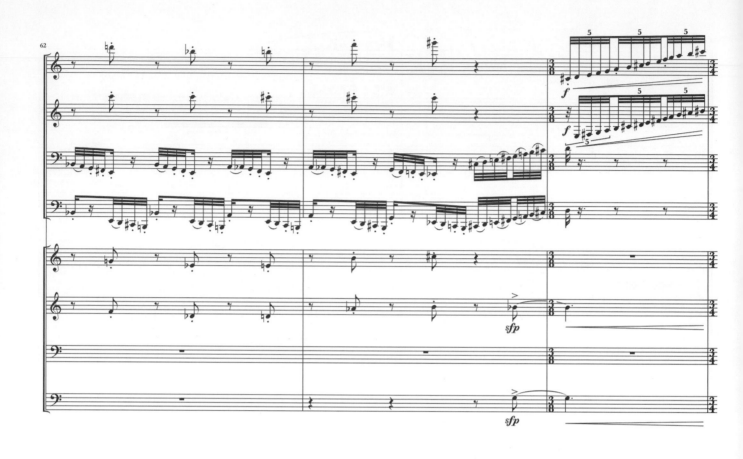

VAR. D ♩ = 160

VAR. A ♪ = 126

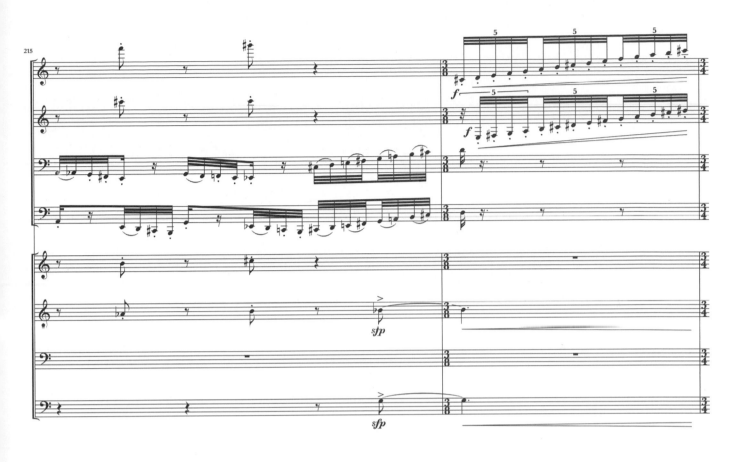

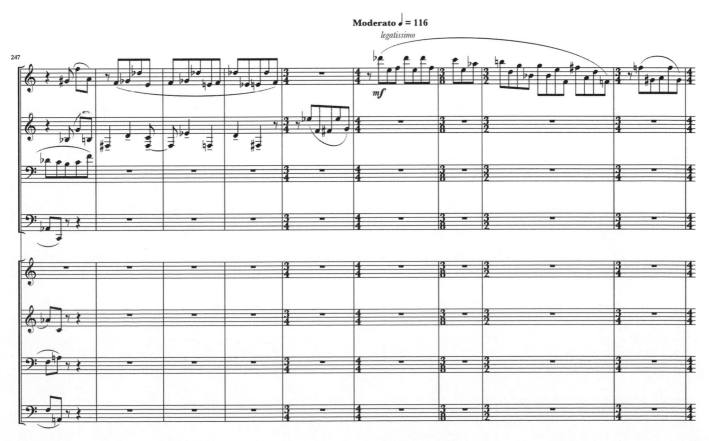

110. *Erlösung,* Op. 18, No. 2 *(1925)*

ANTON WEBERN
(1883–1945)

❖

The row used in this song is almost a "trichordally derived row" (that is one, whose discrete trichords all belong to the same set class). The final trichord, however, differs in set class from the first three. Since Webern's serial technique in this work is fairly easy to follow, what do you make of this "odd trichord out?" Is it used in any particularly effective way for motivic or expressive reasons?

Mary: My child, look upon my soul:
permit no sinner to go astray.

Christ: Mother, look upon the wounds
that I endure every moment for your sins.
Father, grant that my wounds be a sacrifice for all sins.

Father: Son, my dear son,
all that you have asked, shall be.

Translation: Emily Ezust

Sohn, lie - ber Sohn mein, al - - - les, was du be - gehrst, das soll

sein.

111. *Density 21.5*
(1936)

EDGARD VARÈSE
(1883–1965)
❖

The title of this work refers to the density of the metal, platinum, and more specifically to the request made to Varèse by flutist Georges Barrère for a piece of music for the performer's new platinum instrument. Varèse stated that this piece comprises the working out of two central ideas, one modal, the other atonal. Can you hear this, and if so, do you think it would be helpful in memorization and in presentation of the work to an audience?

* Written in January 1936 at the request of Georges Barrère for the inaguration of his platinum flute. Revised April 1946.
21.45 grams per cubic centimeter.

** Always strictly in time—follow metronomic indications.

*** Notes marked + to be played softly, hitting the keys at the same time to produce a percussive effect.

112. Adagio from Concerto for Violin and Orchestra (1935)

ALBAN BERG
(1885–1935)

❖

Written, in part, to commemorate the death of Manon Gropius, daughter of Alma Mahler and her second husband, the Berg violin concerto is a masterpiece of twelve-tone composition. Berg was known for favoring tonal allusions in his choice of row forms and the chords, subsets, and motives he derived from them. The row for the violin concerto features three triads, the last of which overlaps with a whole-tone tetrachord. In the work's final section, this tetrachord is shown to be culled from the opening melodic line of J. S. Bach's chorale "Es ist genug" ("It is enough"). Examine how Berg's use of transformations often results in invariant triads and the whole-tone tetrachord, suggesting a conservative harmonic idiom. Is this triadic structure something to emphasize or deemphasize in performance? Why?

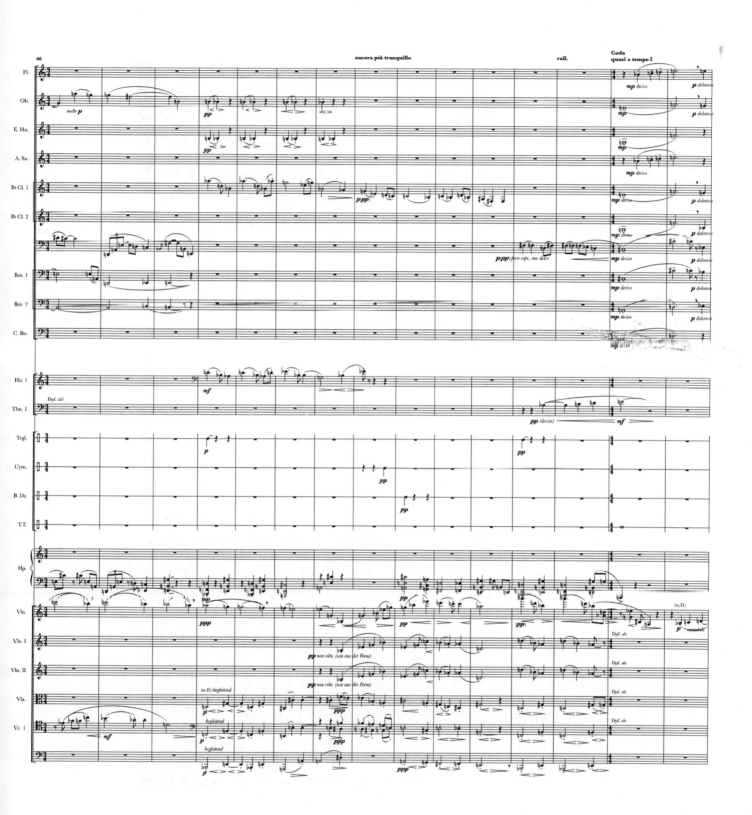

113. Allegro non troppo from
Sextuor Mystique
(1917)

HEITOR VILLA-LOBOS
(1887–1959)

❖

Brazilian composer Heitor Villa-Lobos followed a compositional path taken by many musicians who lived outside the musical mainstream of Central and Western Europe. Like Béla Bartók and others, he blended the folk music of his native country with the Western art-music tradition in pursuing his individual compositional voice. The *Sextuor Mystique* is unique among Villa-Lobos's works in that the composer penned it as a young man, subsequently lost the score, and then rewrote it from memory nearly forty years later!

Quasi allegro

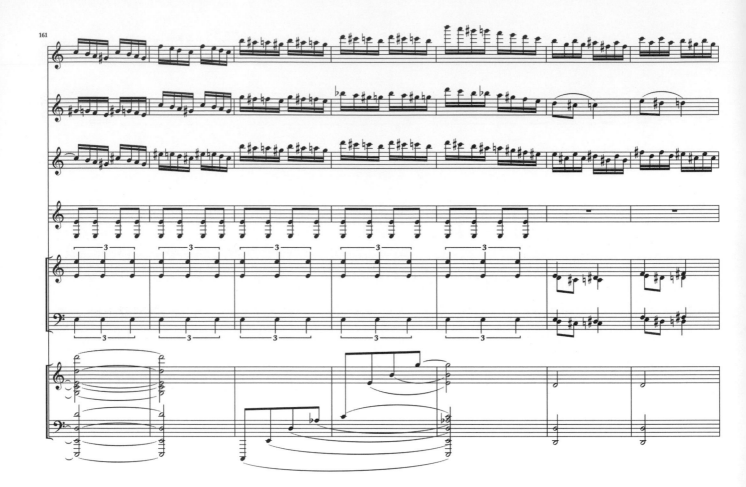

114. "The Montagues and the Capulets" from *Romeo and Juliet* *(1935–36)*

SERGEI PROKOFIEV
(1891–1953)

❖

It was near the end of his years abroad that Prokofiev composed the ballet *Romeo and Juliet*, a story that had also inspired Tchaikovsky, who wrote a fantasy-overture under the title many decades earlier. At the time, Prokofiev was using an apartment in Moscow since he returned frequently to Russia in order to reestablish himself there. The work faced many difficulties in its premiere, being rejected by theaters that thought the music impossible to dance to. Eventually, however, it met with success and is now a staple of both the ballet and concert repertories. Like Tchaikovsky before him, Prokofiev used motto themes throughout the ballet in the manner of Wagnerian leitmotiv. There are fifty-two numbers in the ballet. Rarely are all heard in succession; more often, conductors choose a selection for performance or perform one of Prokofiev's suite arrangements. This number is the opening introduction, which sets the emotional tenor for the story to come.

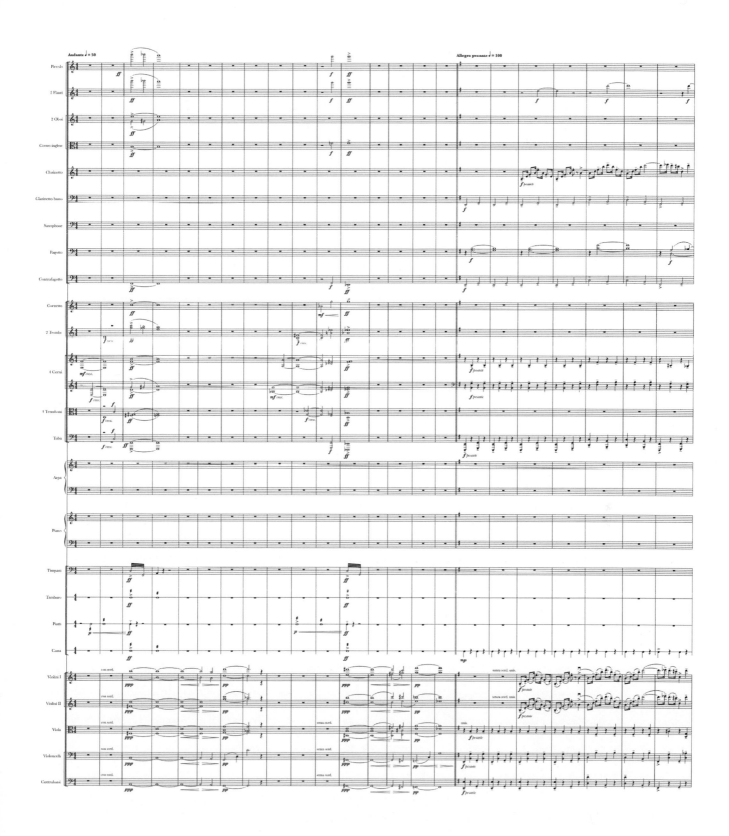

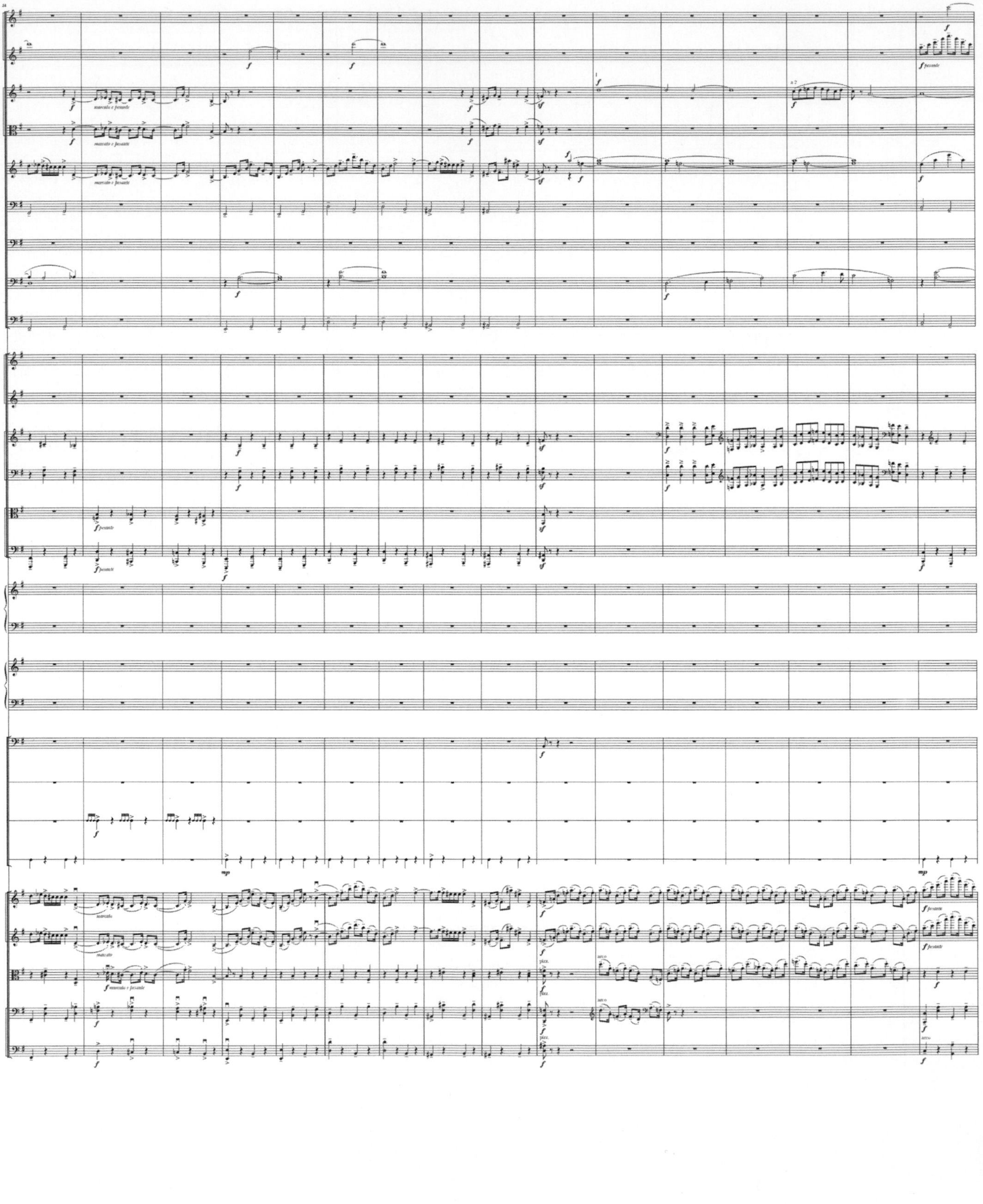
marcato e pesante
f pesante
a 2
marcato
pizz.
arco

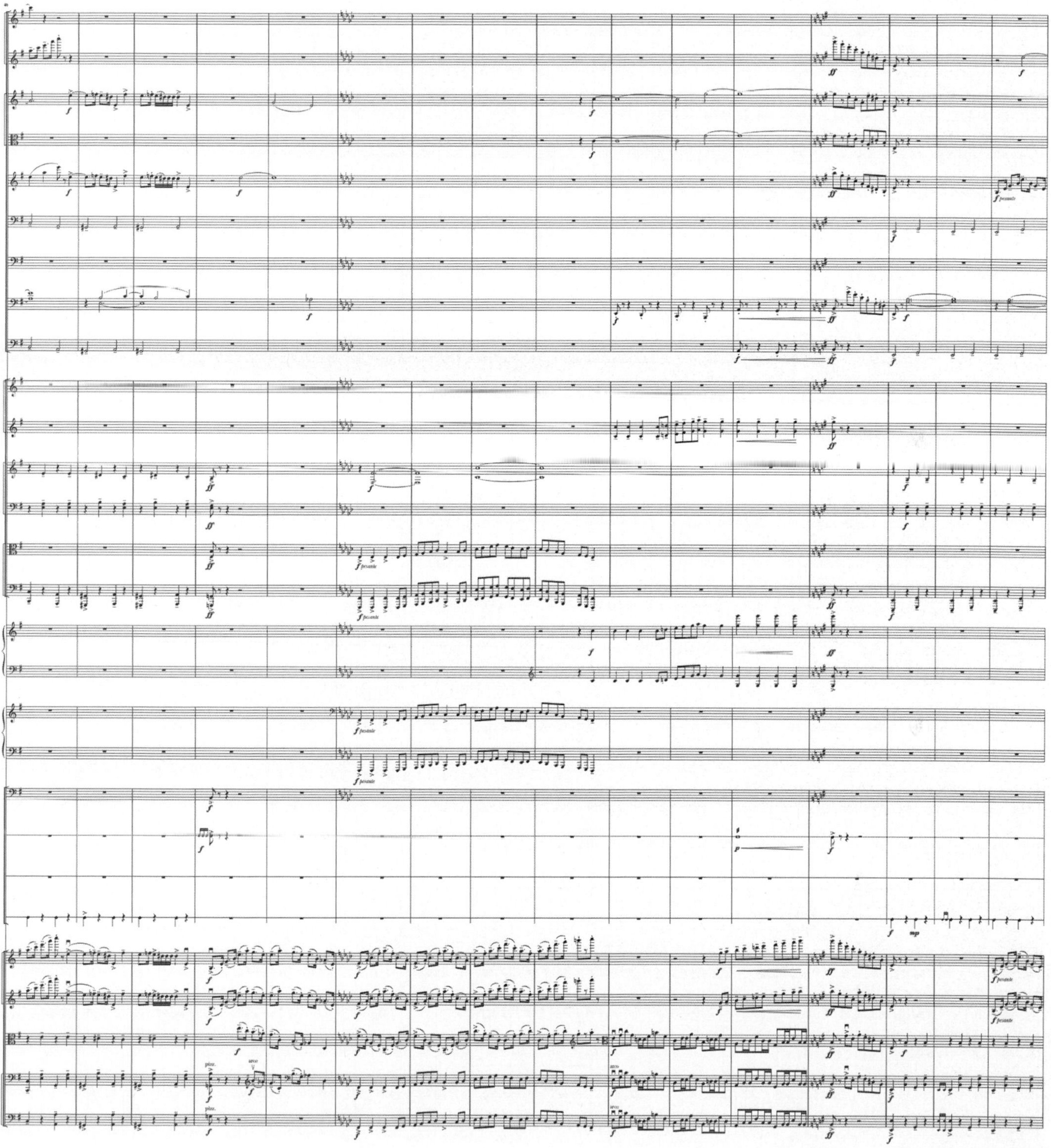
f pesante
pizz.
arco

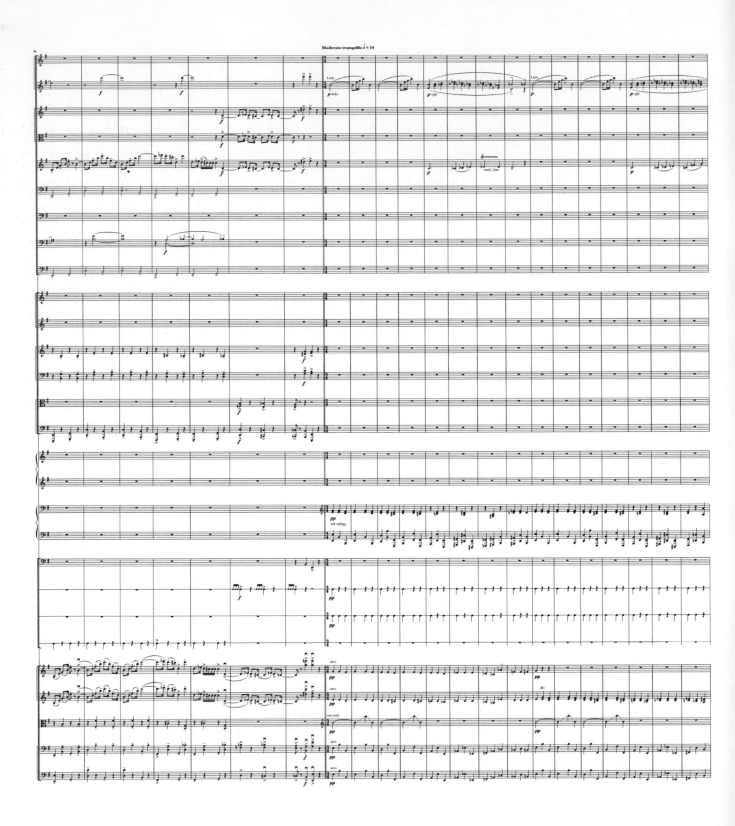

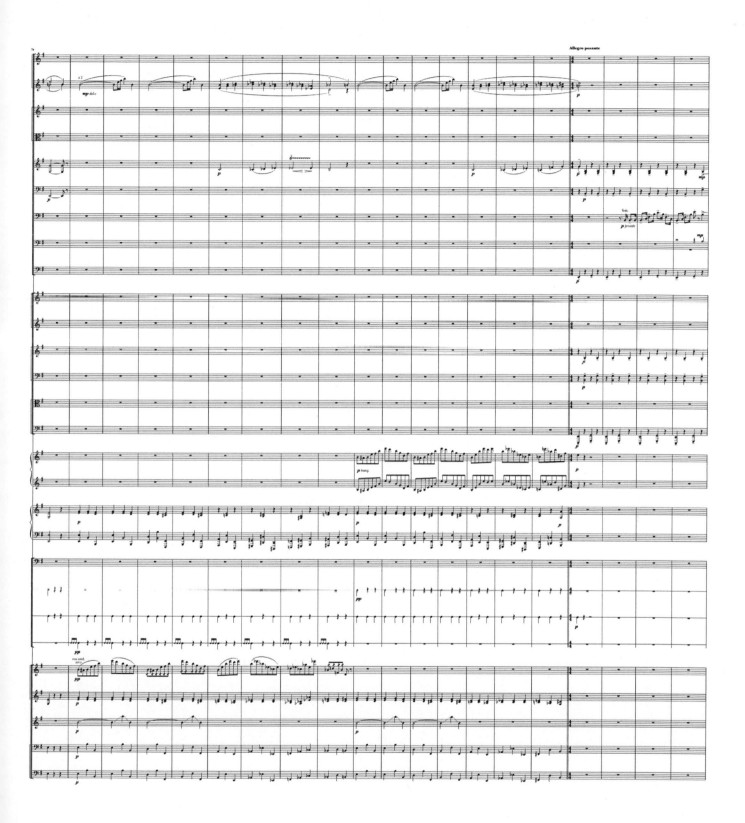

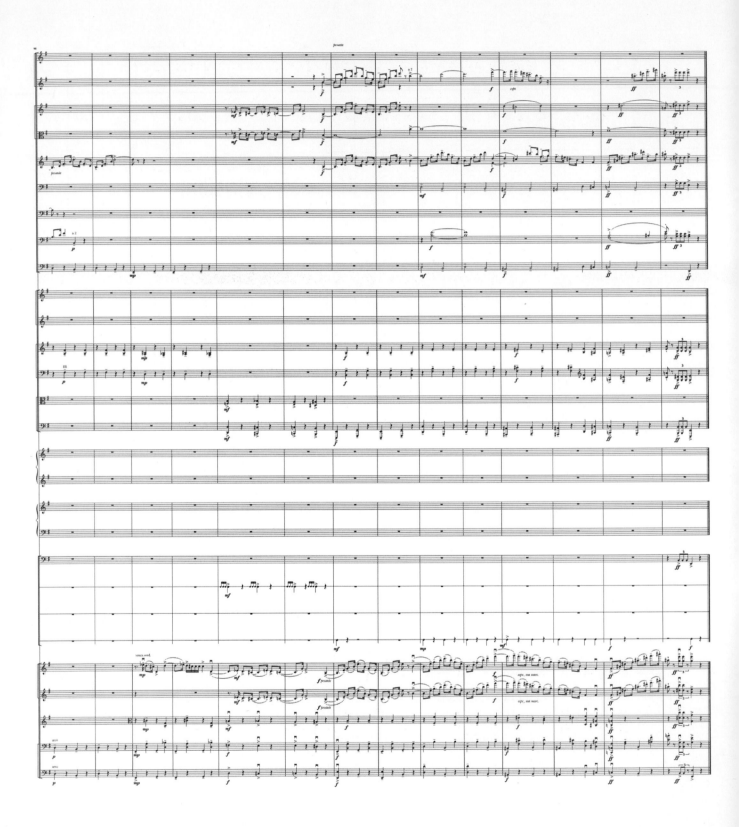

115. *Trauermusik. Sehr langsam* from Sonata for Trumpet and Piano *(1939)*

PAUL HINDEMITH
(1895–1963)
❖

Paul Hindemith set himself the task of writing a series of concerti for all the standard orchestral instruments. He also wrote a parallel series of sonatas for these instruments (most with piano accompaniment) along with instruments such as the English horn and tuba that had been largely ignored by composers writing solo repertory. This work was completed shortly after Hindemith arrived in America, a refugee from Nazi Germany, where his music had been banned for five years.

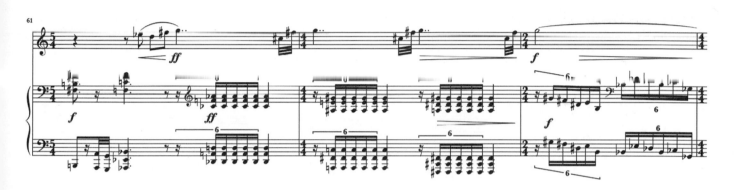

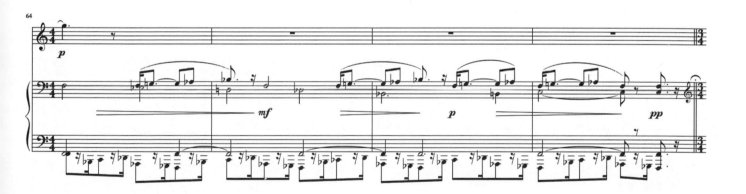

Alle Menschen müssen sterben.

Sehr ruhig (♩ etwa 40)

116. Allegro vivace from *Sextuor* (1932–39)

FRANCIS POULENC
(1899–1963)

❖

Is this work tonal? Certainly, this is a loaded question, since the term *tonal* is broad and vague enough to encompass different meanings. Musicians sometimes speak of "monotonality," "functional tonality," and "centricity" as flavors of tonal practice. Perhaps a better question might be, "In what ways is this work tonal?" How is it not?

Poulenc, Francis (1899–1963), *Allegro vivace* from *Sextuor,* Wilhelm Hansen AS

Subitement, presque le double plus lent sans trainer

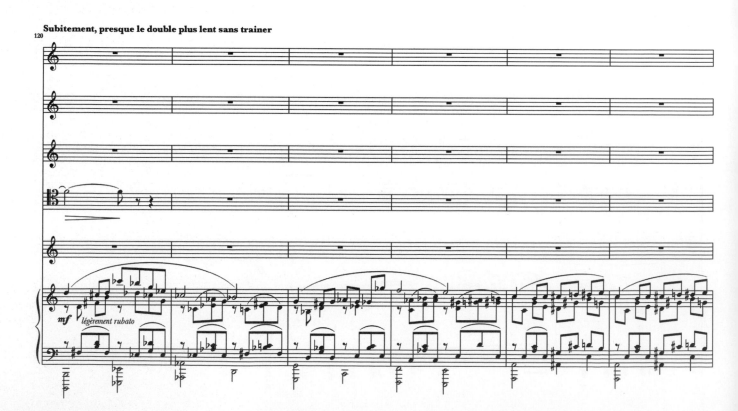

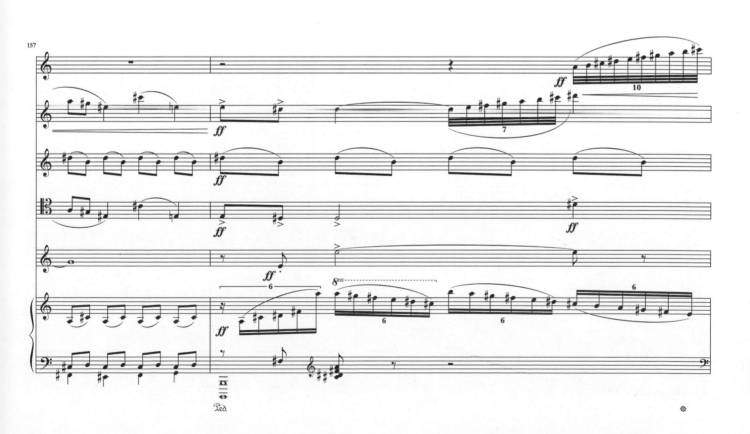

742 ANTHOLOGY FOR ANALYSIS AND PERFORMANCE

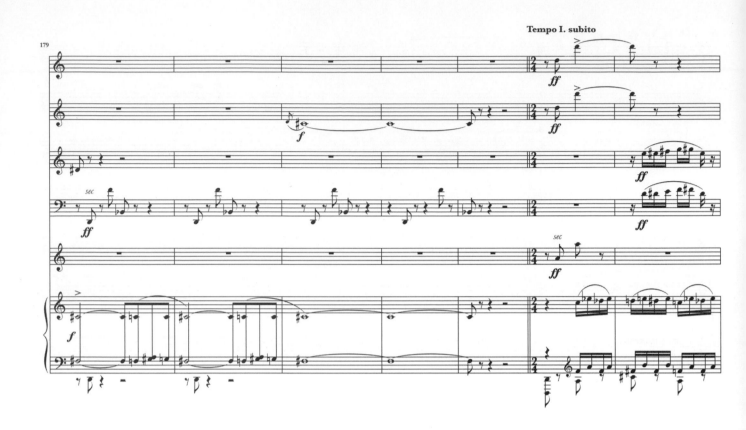

117. Allegretto from Suite for Guitar, Op. 164 (1957)

ERNST KRENEK

(1900–91)

❖

At first glance, the twelve-tone technique in this work seems remarkably simple. The first two phrases, for instance, dutifully plow through the row without any transformations. As the work progresses, though, repetition and interpolation play a large role in modifying the basic row structure. This is a marked departure from the twelve-tone practices of the Second Viennese School (Schoenberg, Webern, and Berg) most often pointed out in the analytic literature: transposition, inversion, retrograde, and use of motivic subsets. How does Krenek's work compare, and what implications does the work's structure have for performance? Being that this is a dance suite, would a convincing performance of this movement as dance influence your structural hearing of the work?

Krenek, Ernst (1900–91), *Allegretto* from Suite for Guitar, Op. 164, Doblinger Musikverlag

118. Allegretto from String Quartet No. 8
(1960)

DMITRI SHOSTAKOVICH
(1906–1975)
❖

Many of Shostakovich's works feature his musical signature: D–Es–C–H (a text-based motive not unlike the signature motives of Schumann or the *soggetti cavati*—literally, "carved subjects," short mottos or motives the composer constructed as the basis of the work—of Renaissance composers). These are the German spellings for the notes D-natural, E-flat, C-natural, and B-natural, the opening of the Allegretto movement from the Eighth String Quartet. What role does the signature motive have to play in the remainder of the movement?

Shostakovich, Dmitri (1906–75), *Allegretto* from String Quartet No. 8, G. Schirmer

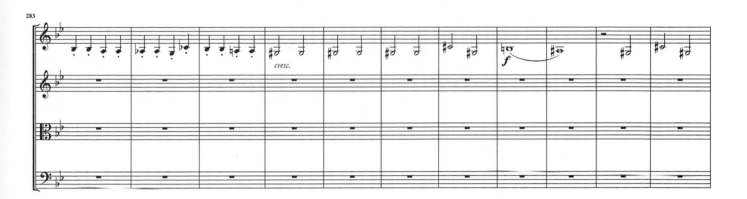

119. *Vocalise pour l'Ange qui annonce le fin du Temps* from *Quatuor pour le fin du temps* *(1940–41)*

OLIVIER MESSIAEN
(1908–92)
❖

This work is regarded by many as the quintessence of Messiaen's compositional voice. It was inspired both by profound events in the composer's life (namely the time he spent with a clarinetist, violinist, and cellist while the four men were prisoners of the Germans during World War II) and by the composer's faith (specifically, passages from the Book of Revelation). The second movement also evokes the composer's famed synaesthesia, in which sounds, quite literally, evoke colors.

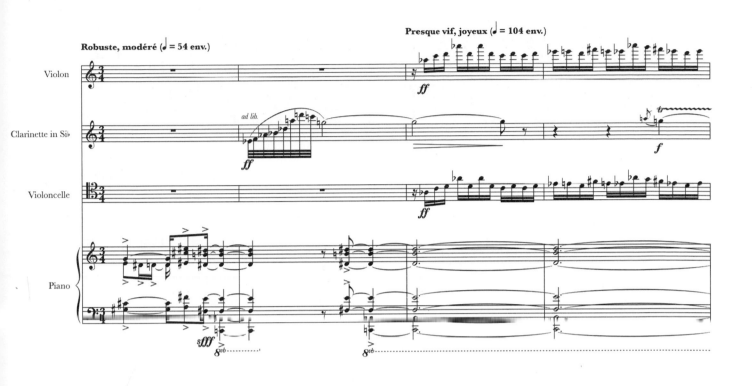

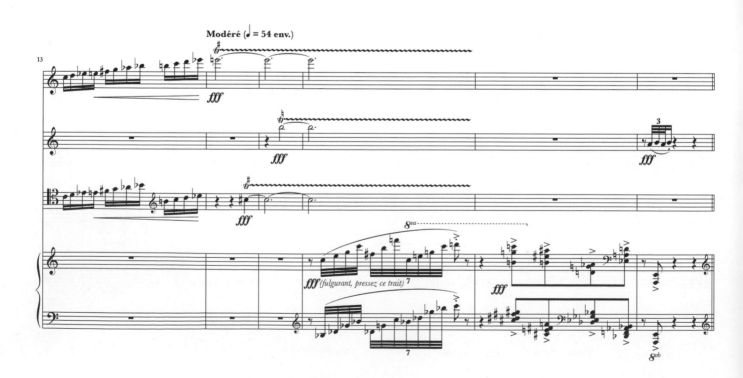

Presque lent, impalpable, lontain (♪ = 50 env.)

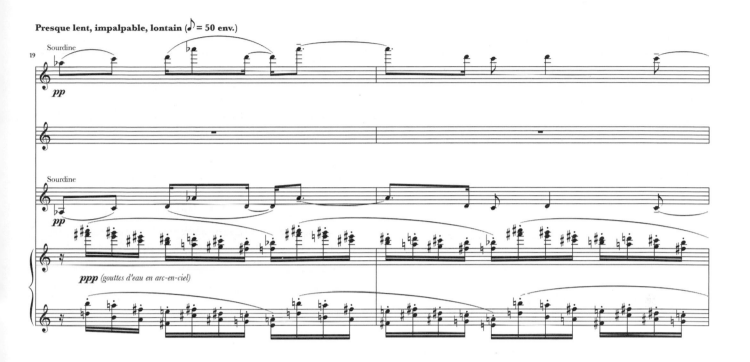

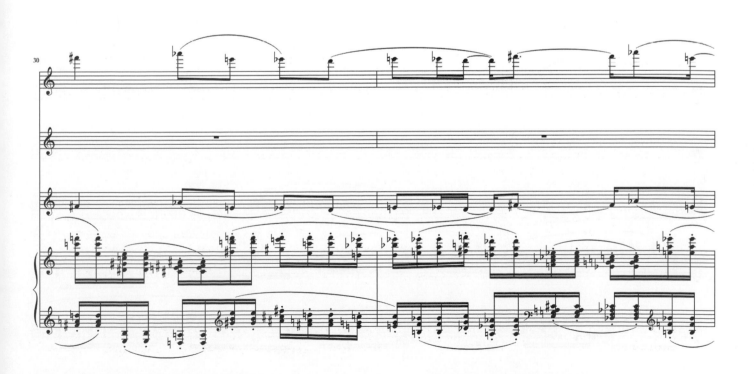

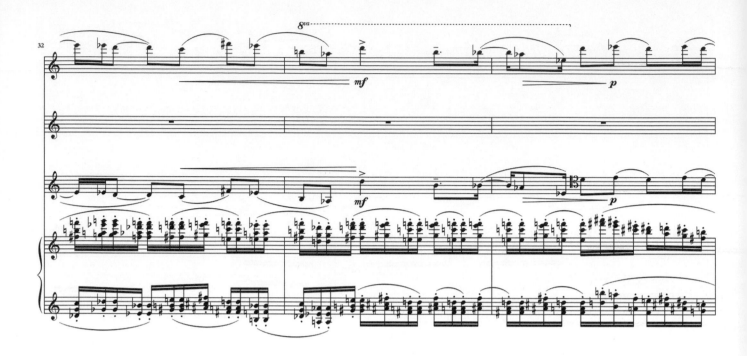

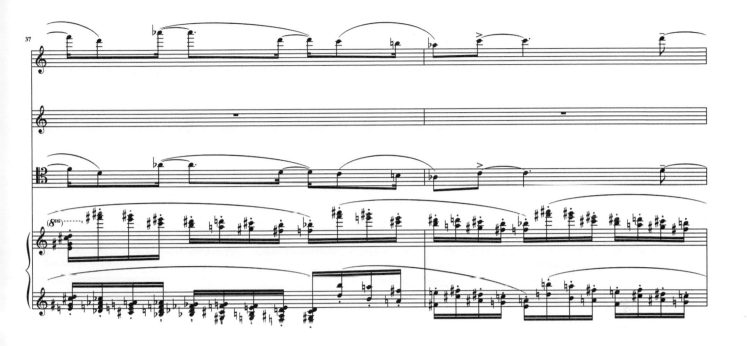

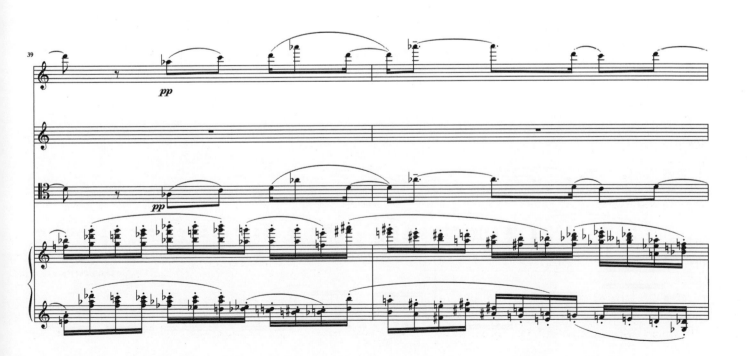

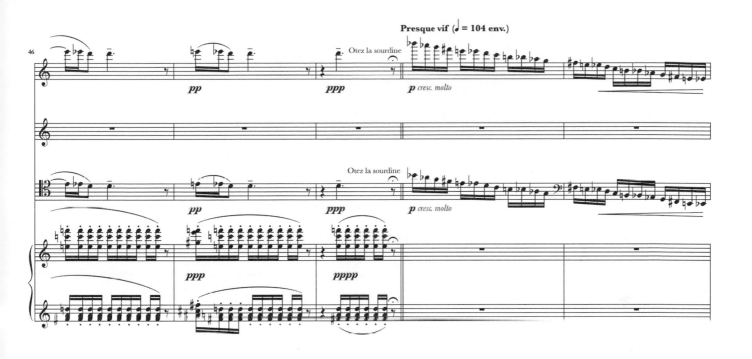

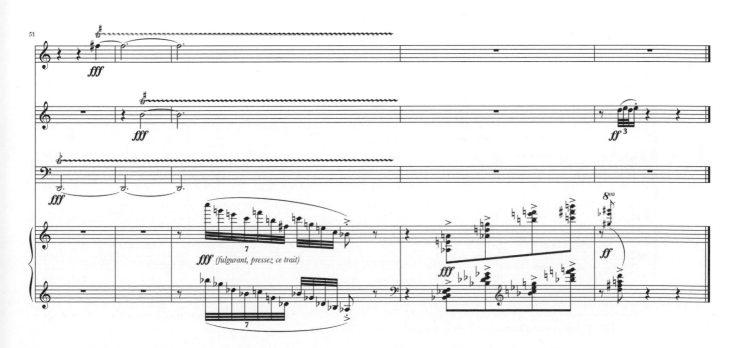

120. Introduction from String Quartet No. 2 *(1959)*

ELLIOTT CARTER
(1908–2012)
❖

At the writing of this anthology, American composer Elliott Carter was still alive, an active creator of music at the advanced age of 103! Carter's life and career stretch back throughout American history; he studied for a time with Charles Ives and in turn influenced dozens, if not hundreds, of composers and theorists working in the second half of the twentieth century.

Carter's contributions to American music and culture were recognized in 1960 when he won the Pulitzer Prize (among others) for his second string quartet. Doubtless, part of this work's appeal stems from Carter's treatment of the four instruments (two violins, viola, and cello), each of which adopts a personality or temperament that is expressed musically throughout the quartet; thus audiences witness a musical conversation among four individuals. In service to this idea, each instrument has characteristic rhythmic gestures, articulations, and musical intervals, all of which are evident in the Introduction to the work.

Carter, **Elliott** (1908–), *Introduction* from String Quartet No. 2, G. Schirmer

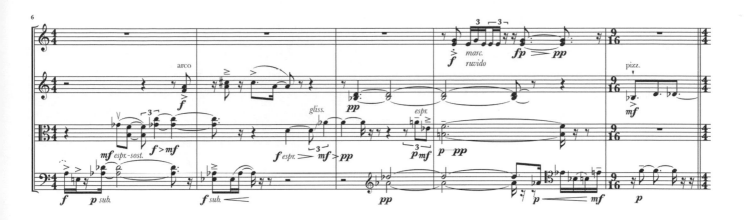

Subito meno mosso (♩ = 112)

121. Excerpt from *Shard*
(1997)

ELLIOTT CARTER
(1908–2012)
❖

Shard's title is not misleading; the work is indeed a "splinter" of another longer work for solo guitar—*Luimen*—which contains all of *Shard* save its last chord. *Shard* is exemplary of Carter's best-known metric technique: metric modulation. Note how tempo changes and note values relate to one another throughout the work.

122. Moderato from *Diversion* for Alto Saxophone and Band *(1943)*

BERNHARD HEIDEN
(1910–2000)
❖

Bernhard Heiden studied composition at Yale with Paul Hindemith. His works are well known to wind players, especially those whose focus tends more toward the band, rather than the orchestral, tradition. Heiden's orientation toward concert band and wind music and his conservative tonal language have resulted in his standing largely outside the narrative of musical history. As you analyze this work, what about it seems conservative or traditional?

Heiden, Bernhard (1910–2000), Moderato from Diversion for Alto Saxophone and Band, © Keiser Classical (BMI). Used by permission.

123. *Dolente* from Double Concerto for Oboe, Harpsichord, and Chamber Orchestra *(1980)*

WITOLD LUTOSLAWSKI
(1913–94)

Many of Witold Lutoslawski's mature works combine two hallmarks of twentieth-century art-music composition: chance and dissonant counterpoint. The combination of imitative lines at random (actually, performer-selected) time intervals is a technique known as aleatoric counterpoint. How does one go about analyzing such music? What implications does it have for the importance of consonance and dissonance in contrapuntal practice?

Lutoslawski, Witold (1913–94), *Dolente* from Double Concerto for Oboe, Harp, and Chamber Orchestra. University of Minnesota.

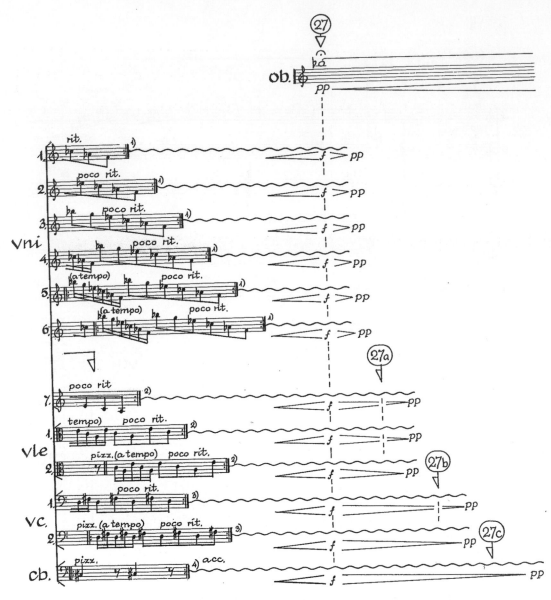

1. Repeat until ㉗ , then play to the end of the repeated phrase and stop.
2. Repeat until ㉗ₐ , then play to the end of the repeated phrase and stop.
3. Repeat until ㉗ᵦ , then play to the end of the repeated phrase and stop.
4. Repeat until ㉗ᵧ , then play to the end of the repeated phrase and stop.

1. Bis ㉗ wiederholen, dann bis zum Ende der Phrase spielen und aufhören.
2. Bis ㉗ₐ wiederholen, dann bis zum Ende der Phrase spielen und aufhören.
3. Bis ㉗ᵦ wiederholen, dann bis zum Ende der Phrase spielen und aufhören.
4. Bis ㉗ᵧ wiederholen, dann bis zum Ende der Phrase spielen und aufhören.

1. The conductor has been following the oboe part. He gives a sign to the harp who plays up to the :|| and then stops.

1. Der Dirigent folgte der Oboenstimme, und gibt hier der Harfe ein Zeichen, welche bis zum :|| spielt, und aufhört.

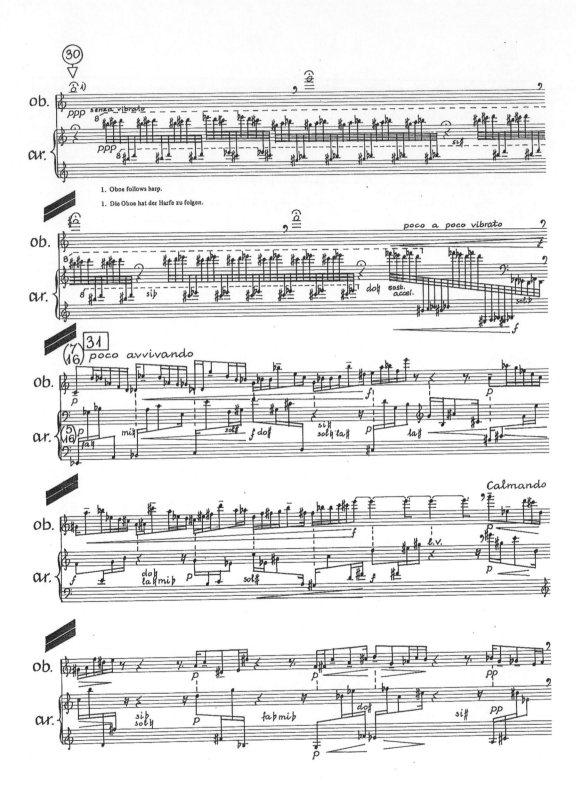

1. Oboe follows harp.

1. Die Oboe hat der Harfe zu folgen.

1. Repeat, getting slower and softer until the oboe phrase ends.
2. Begin as soon as the oboe phrase has finished.

1. Immer langsamer und leiser wiederholen bis zum Ende der Oboenphrase.
2. Anfangen sobald die Oboenphrase zu Ende ist.

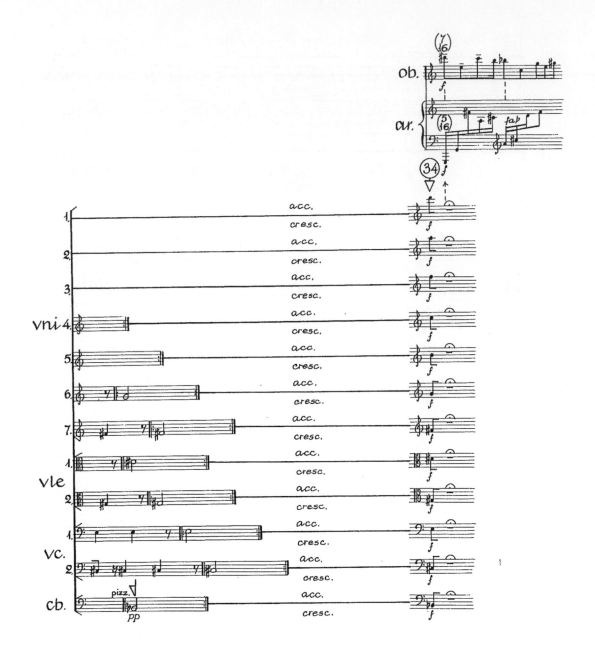

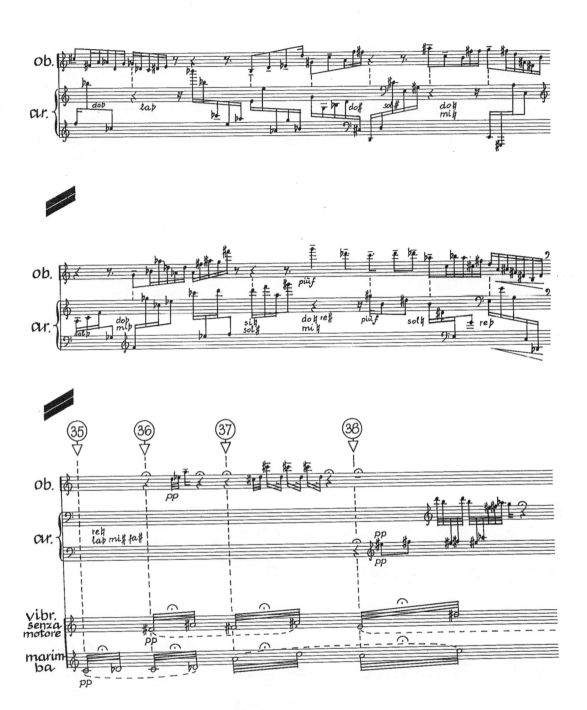

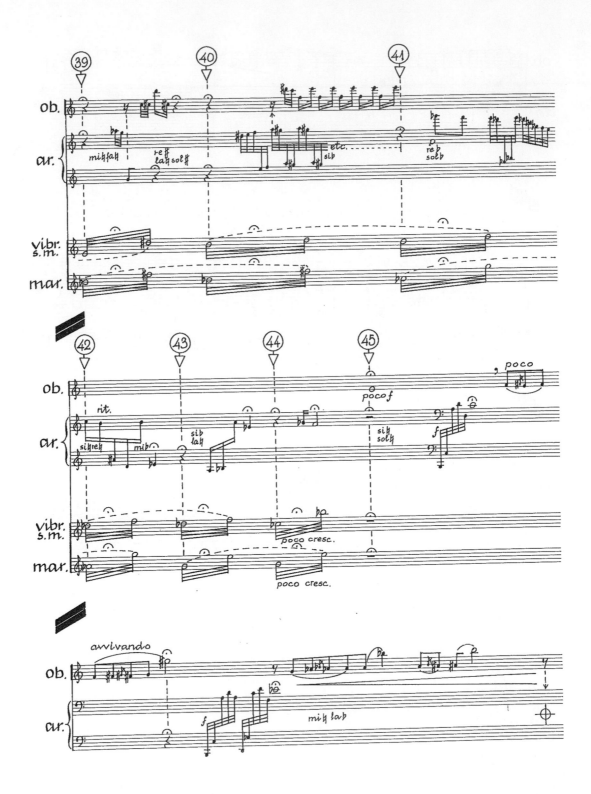

1. From here until ㊼ , the oboe and harp each play independently.
2. The conductor follows the harp.

1. Von hier bis ㊼ spielen die Oboe und die Harfe unabhängig von einander.
2. Der Dirigent folgt der Harfe.

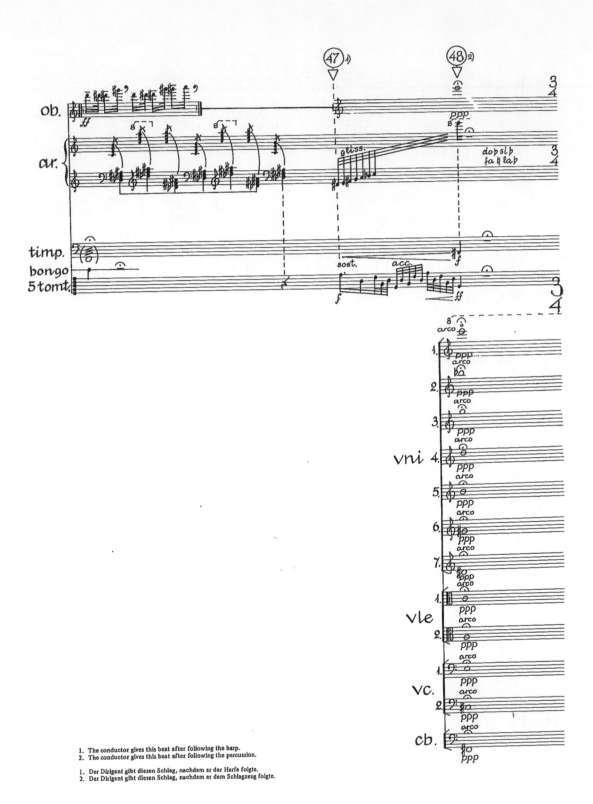

1. The conductor gives this beat after following the harp.
2. The conductor gives this beat after following the percussion.

1. Der Dirigent gibt diesen Schlag, nachdem er der Harfe folgte.
2. Der Dirigent gibt diesen Schlag, nachdem er dem Schlagzeug folgte.

1. All glissandi start at the beginning of the note.

1. Alle Glissandi beginnen am Anfang der Note.

attacca

124. *Parable XXII* for Tuba
(1981)

VINCENT PERSICHETTI
(1915–1987)
❖

Persichetti's parables could be described as "gestural" music. Gestures as we know them are embodied phenomena with shape, duration, and often meaningful implications. There is a danger, however, in conceiving of gestural art since one might be tempted to focus only on the local level and small scale. On the other hand, do we make more of such works than they deserve if we search for long-range and large-scale processes and connections? How do gestures combine to create a larger sense of a cohesive form? Or do they need to?

125. Excerpt from *Whirled Series* for Alto Saxophone and Piano *(1987)*

MILTON BABBITT
(1916–2011)

❖

As the name implies, this is a serialist work. Given the number of twelve-tone pieces included in this anthology, it might be possible to start appreciating their variety. This one is beholden to both the jazz and neoclassical movements in the twentieth century.

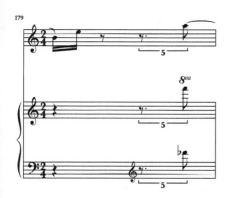

126. *Andante tranquillo ed un poco rubato* from Duo for Oboe and Bassoon *(1979)*

GEORGE ROCHBERG
(1918–2005)
❖

The second movement of George Rochberg's Duo for Oboe and Bassoon is a canon. The writing differs, however, from that of Renaissance-, Baroque-, and Classic-era contrapuntalists in that the strict treatment of dissonance (namely, its preparation and resolution) is greatly relaxed. In addition to Rochberg, twentieth-century composers such as Shostakovich, Hindemith, Lutoslawski, and Ruth Crawford Seeger are known for writing this "dissonant" counterpoint. In some of these works there are still dissonance treatments; they just vary from tonal practice. In others, there are not. Which holds true for this work? Does dissonance seem to be at all prepared or resolved? If so, how does it differ from the earlier counterpoint of a composer such as Palestrina or Bach?

Andante tranquillo ed un poco rubato

127. *Mists*
(1981)

IANNIS XENAKIS
(1922–2001)

❖

The idea of chance in musical composition and performance occupied many musicians in the decades after World War II. Some composers selected notes, rhythms, timbres, articulations, and so forth by chance when they composed. Others determined their musical materials but left the selection of which parts would be performed or when they would be performed up to the performers or to some other chance phenomenon. And composers such as Iannis Xenakis wrote *stochastic* music in which chance is not involved in the composition or performance of the work, but the end effect is meant to conjure up natural processes like the Brownian motion of gasses—processes that may have causal explanations but that often strike human perceivers as governed by chance. What is it about *Mists* that creates this impression of stochastic process?

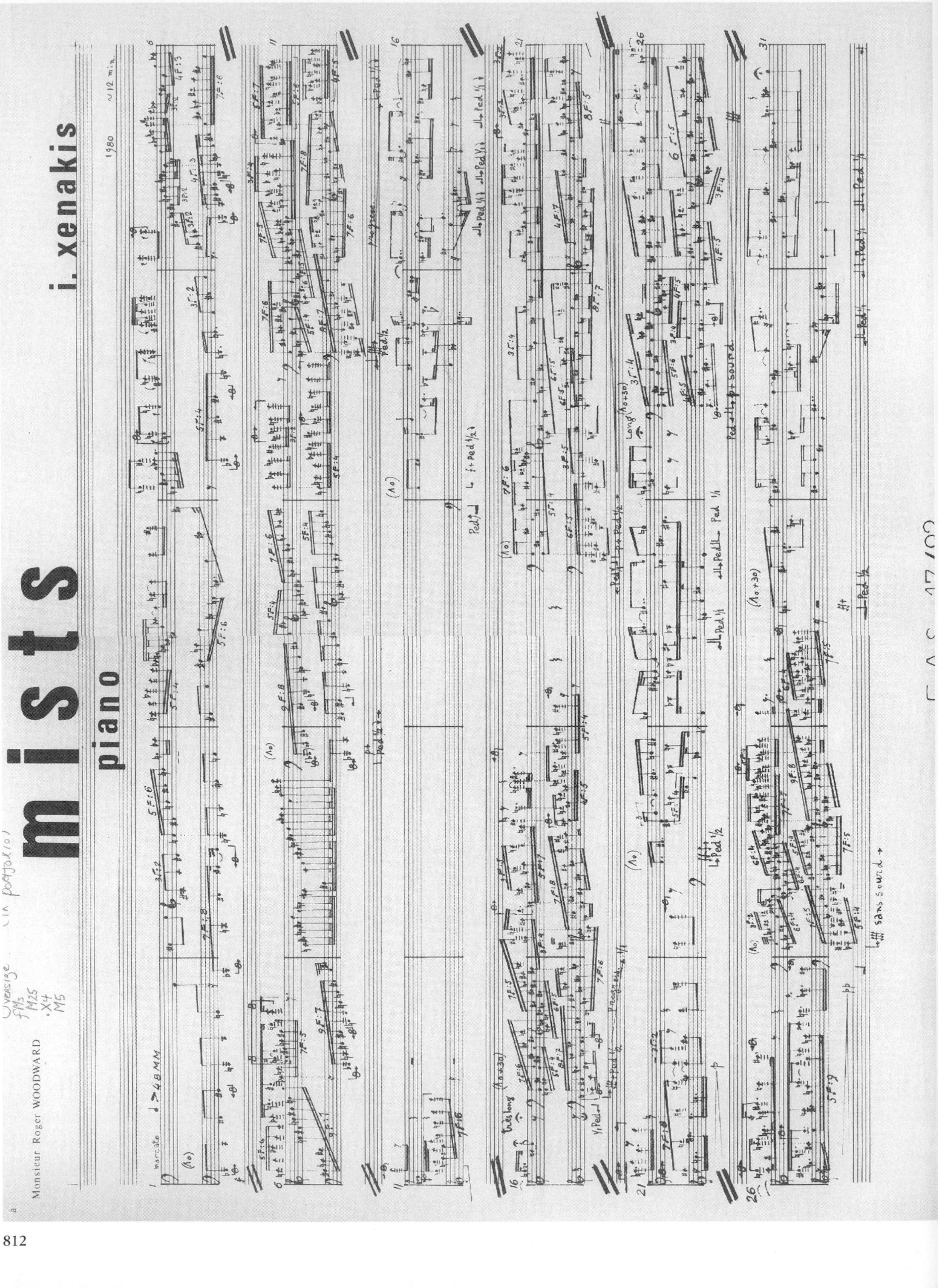
mists
piano
i. xenakis
Monsieur Roger WOODWARD
1980
~12 min.
marcato
♪ > 48 MM
très long
Long
sans sourd.
progress.

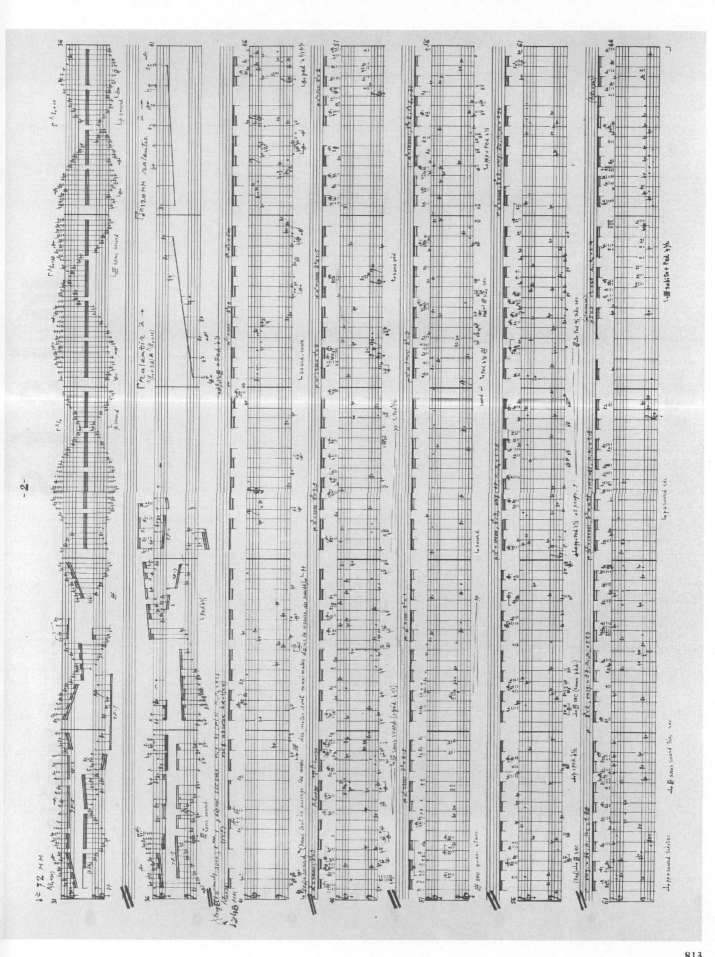

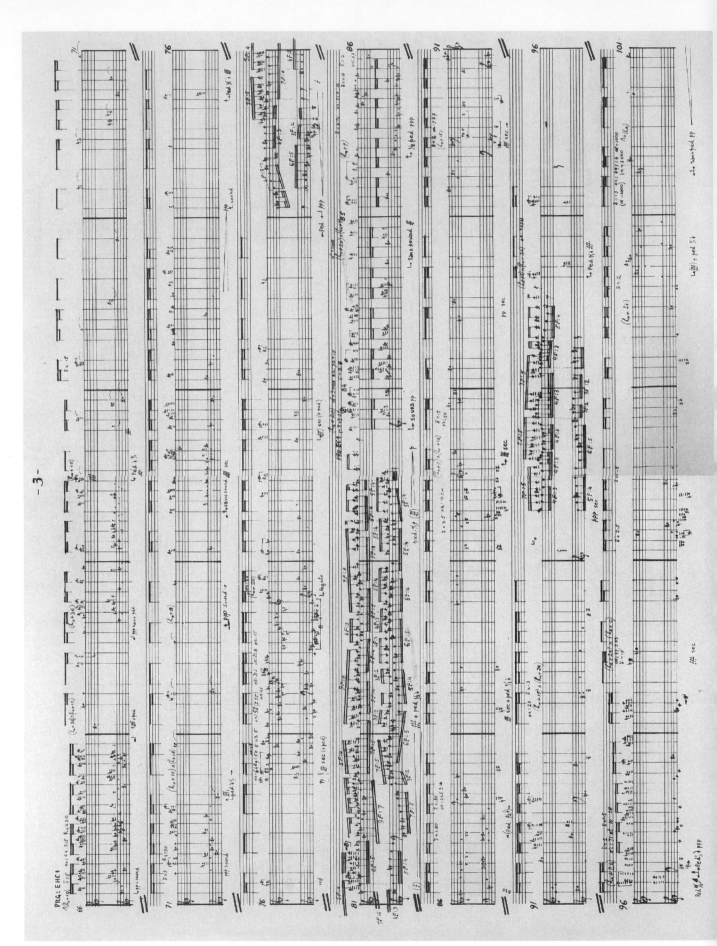

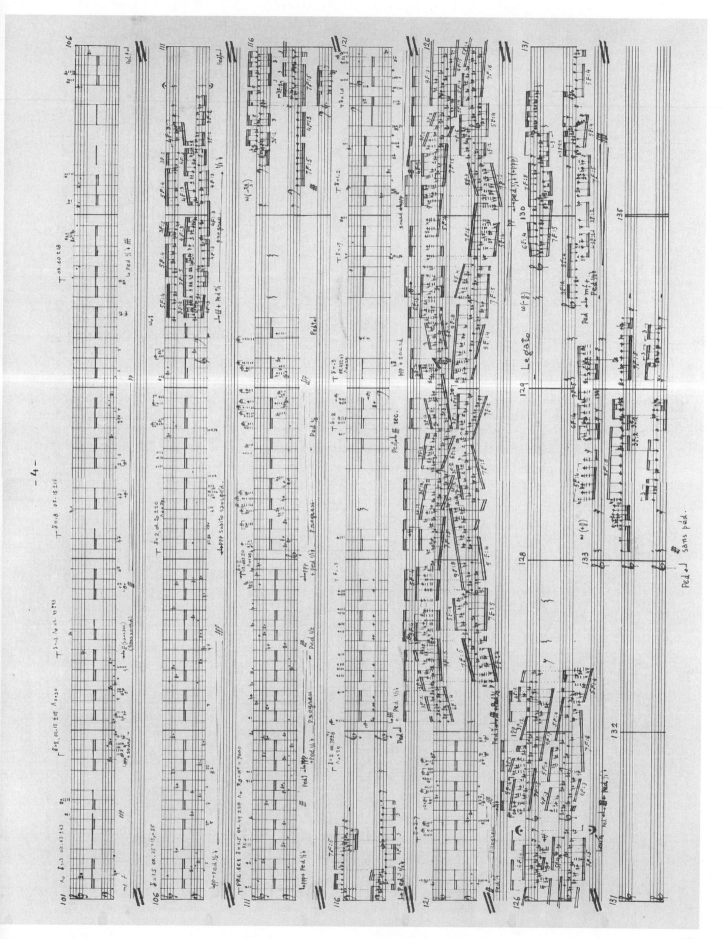

128. *Lento* from Ten Pieces for Wind Quintet *(1968)*

GYÖRGY LIGETI
(1923–2006)

❖

Many of Ligeti's works are process-oriented. What might that mean for this work? Is the process pitch-oriented? Rhythmically oriented? Texturally oriented? Some combination of these?

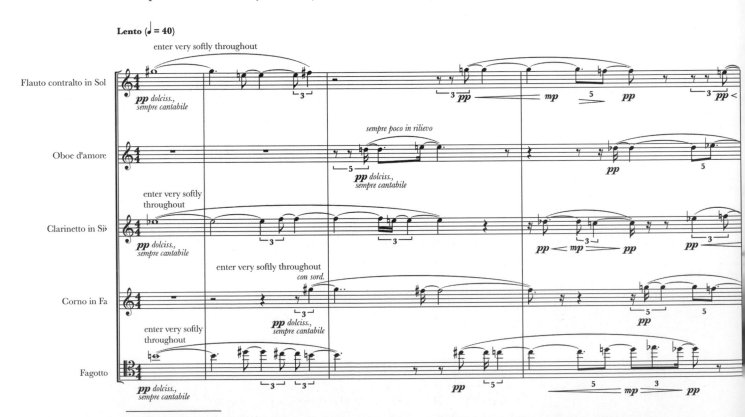

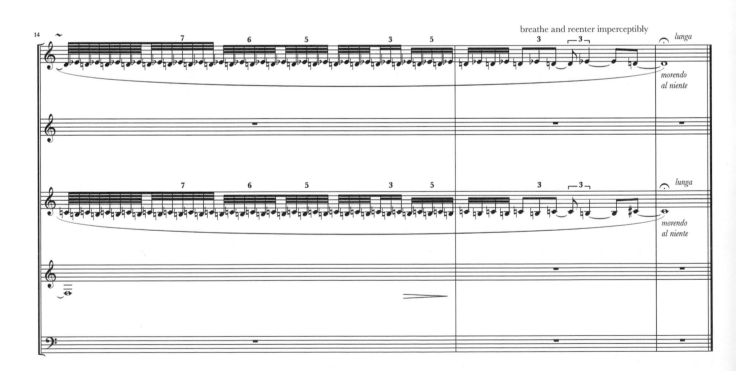

129. *Allegro nervoso* from String Quartet No. 2 *(1968)*

GYÖRGY LIGETI
(1923–2006)
❖

György Ligeti always embraced individualism. One sees this trait in his political and life choices (after surviving the Nazi and Stalinist regimes, he left Hungary when faced with yet another repressive governing body after Russia forcibly quashed Hungary's independence movement in 1956). One also sees it in his music. After struggling against the musical mainstream in Eastern Europe, Ligeti flouted the musical avant-garde in Western Europe. Rather than embracing serialism, he sought musical innovation in an individual way, as is evident in the wide range of styles and compositional techniques his output displays. Near the end of his career, when many of the musical advances he had embraced (such as ostinatos and postmodernist retrospective) had become almost commonplace, Ligeti turned once more against the mainstream and sought inspiration from the neglected Caribbean, central African, and East Asian musical traditions.

In the Second String Quartet, we see Ligeti flirting with futurism. (The third movement is expressly evocative of machinery and clockwork in particular.) Futurism as an artistic movement is usually considered an Italian phenomenon of the early-to-middle twentieth century. (It was also adopted by the Russian musical avant-garde of this time.) Its focus centered on speed, machinery, technology, industry, and the violence to humankind that these forces wrought in the modern world, and its effects are visible not only in musical composition but also in literature, visual arts, cooking, fashion, and interior design.

In the Western art tradition, experiments in futurism led to many compositional approaches associated with midcentury music. These include not only a fascination with mechanical sounds like those in Ligeti's quartet but also the use of any sound (including everyday noise) as music, total serialism, extended vocal techniques, graphic notation, improvisation, and minimalism.

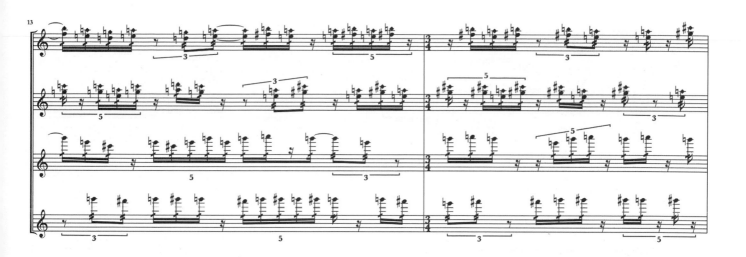

(natürlich Flageolett-Töne, selbst
wenn sie schlecht ansprechen)

(die Obertönen 7. und 8.
erklingen andeutungsweise)

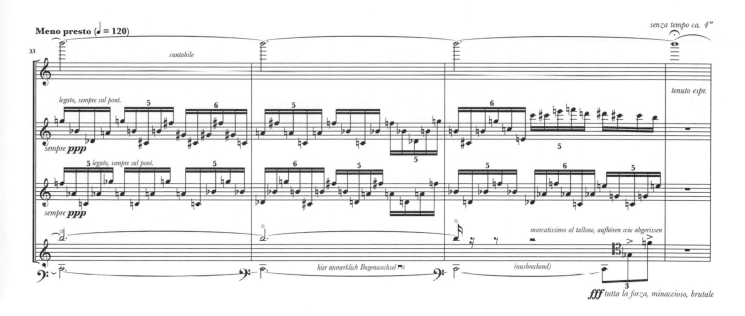

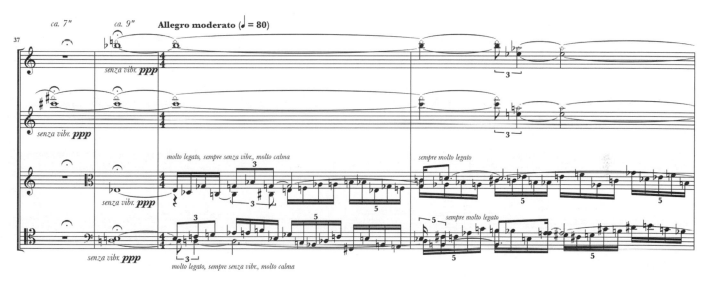

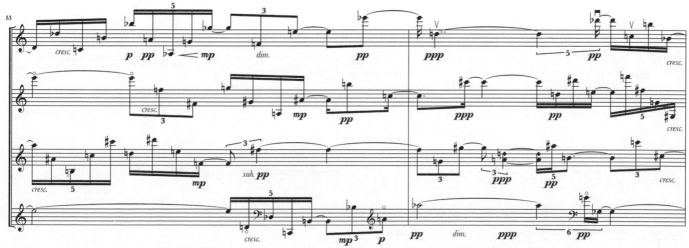

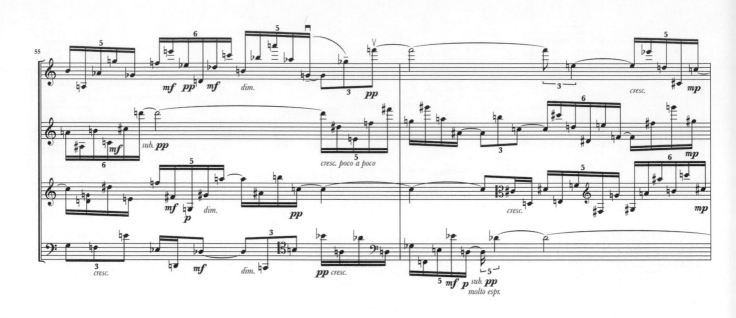

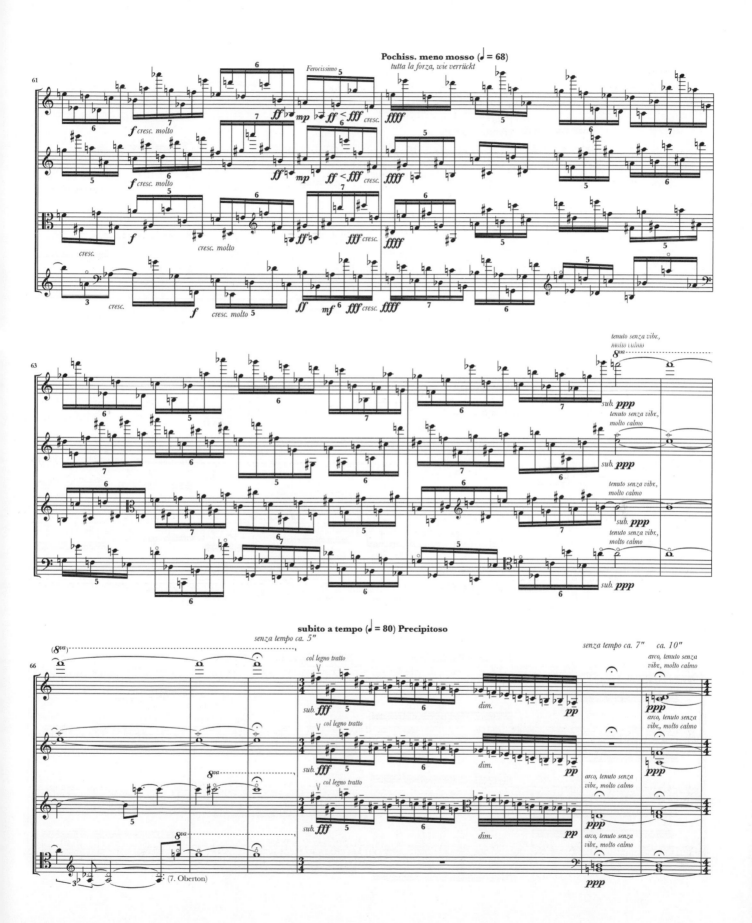

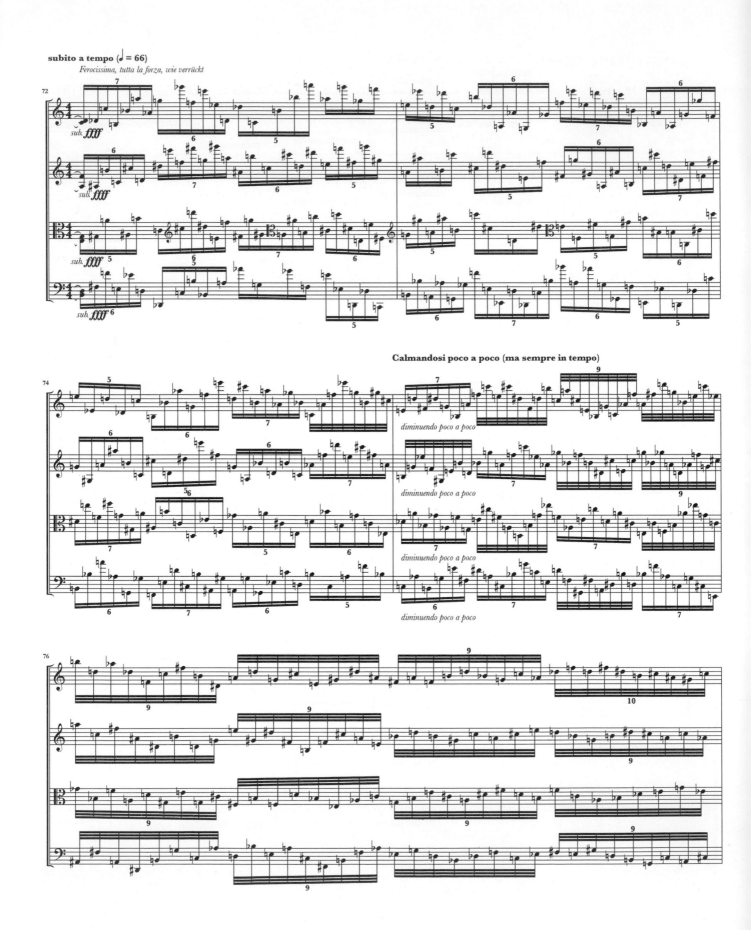

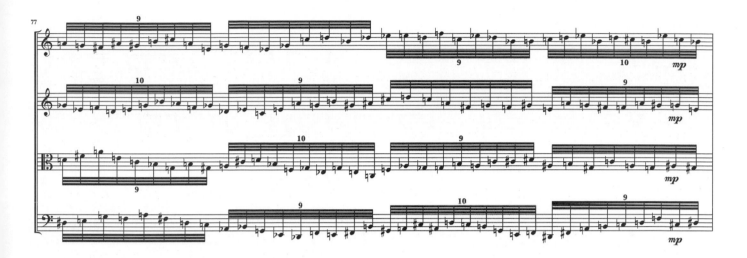

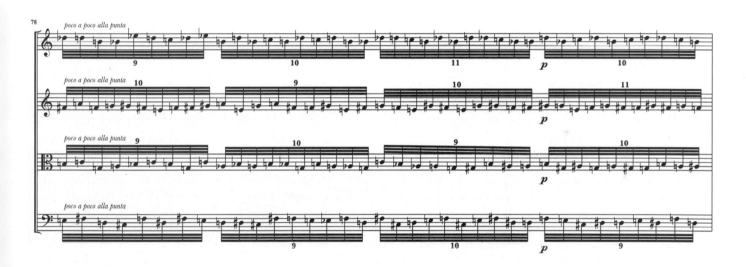

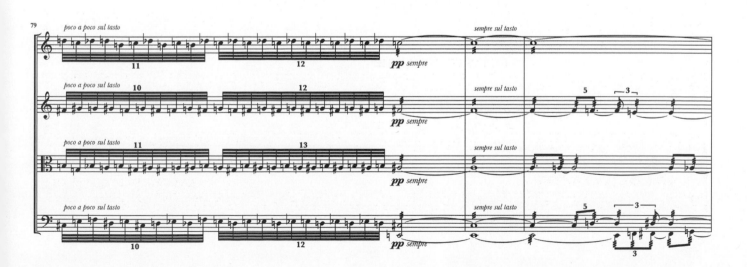

(Alle Instrumente Takt 84): Quasi legato vom Tremolo
zum Flageolett: Von hier ab: Legatissimo Strich für Strich
sin al fine. Sempre senza vibrato, molto calmo.

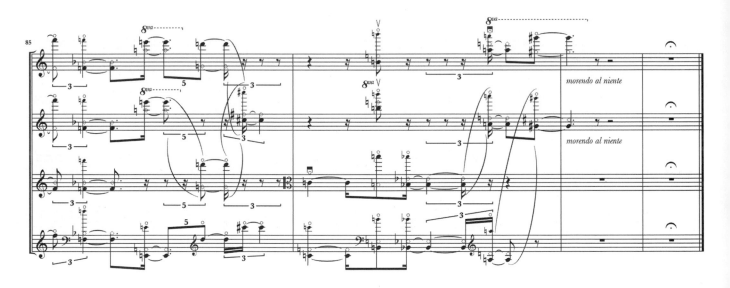

130. *Psy*
(1989)

LUCIANO BERIO
(1925–2003)
❖

Psy, for solo double bass, is not characteristic of Luciano Berio's compositional output, which is most often noted for its use of electronic sound manipulation and the adaptation of preexisting music. *Psy* is, however, a good example of the stylistic diversity many twentieth-century composers pursued. A number of composers felt no allegiance to one particular school of composition to the exclusion of all others. Does this work remind you at all of the Bach cello suite movement or the Bartók string quartet movement included in this anthology? In what ways? One might hear this work as governed by dyads (i.e., interval classes). Can one speak of it as process-oriented with regard to two-note intervals?

131. *dérive*
(1984)

PIERRE BOULEZ
(1925–)
❖

The title of this piece translates as "derivative" and refers not only to the work as being derived from two of Boulez's earlier works (*Répons* and *Messagesquisse*) but also to the structure of the work, which is a variation of sorts on rotation of six chords. The choral rotation is intended as an homage to the Swiss musician Paul Sacher. Do the six letters in Sacher's last name seem to have any relationship to Boulez's compositional choices?

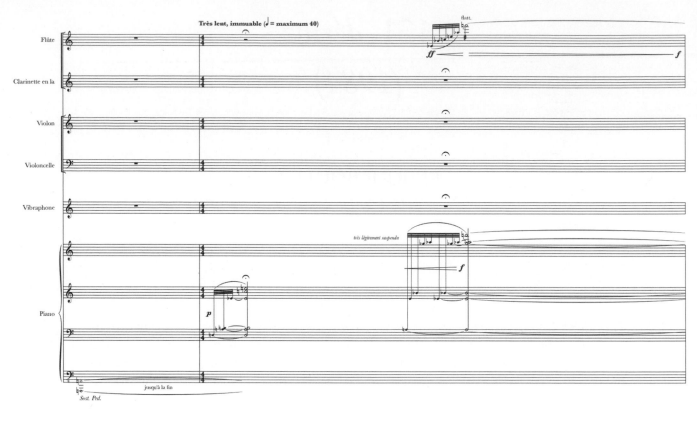

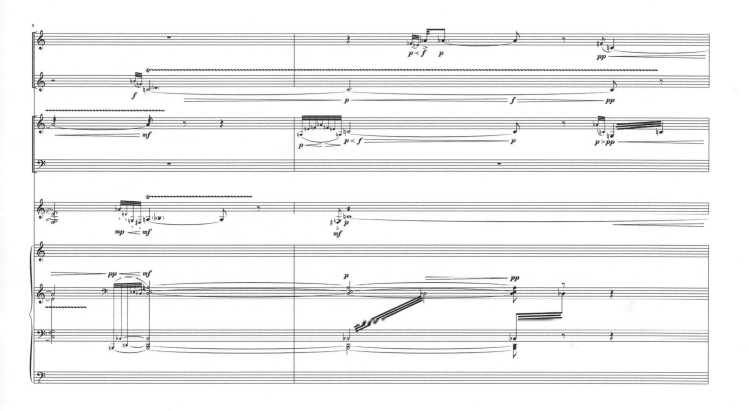

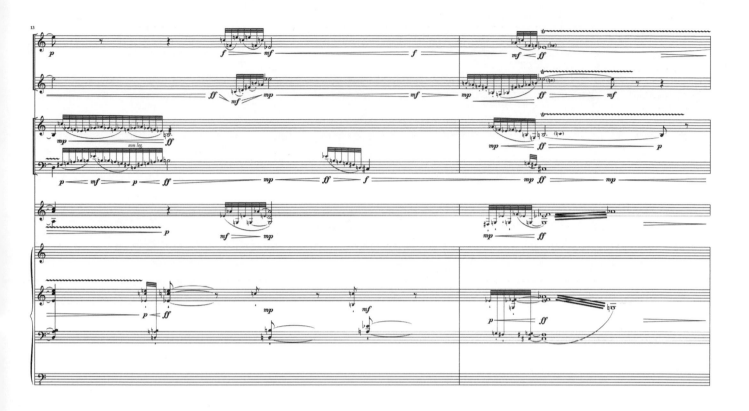

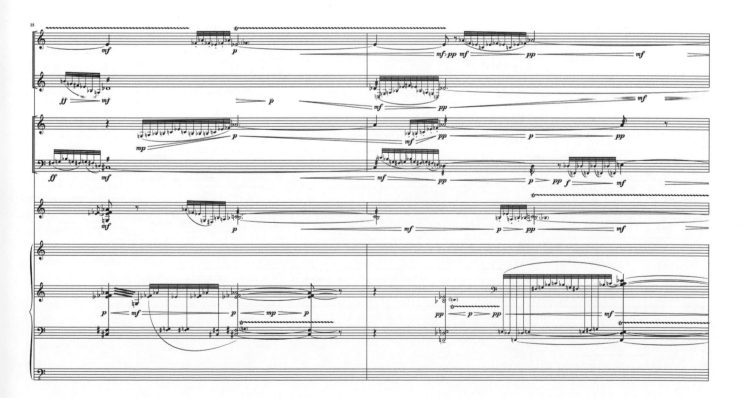

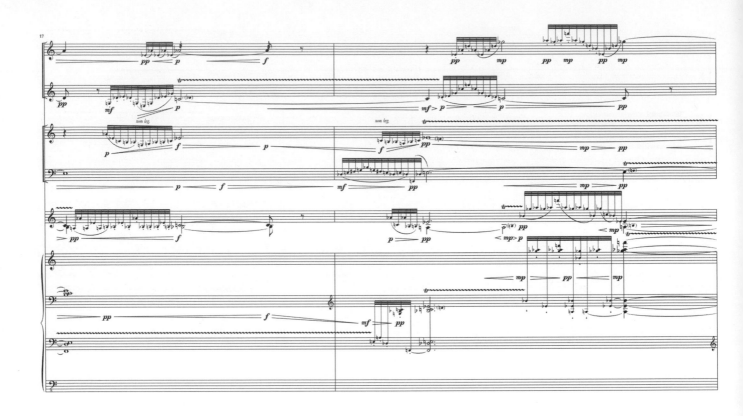

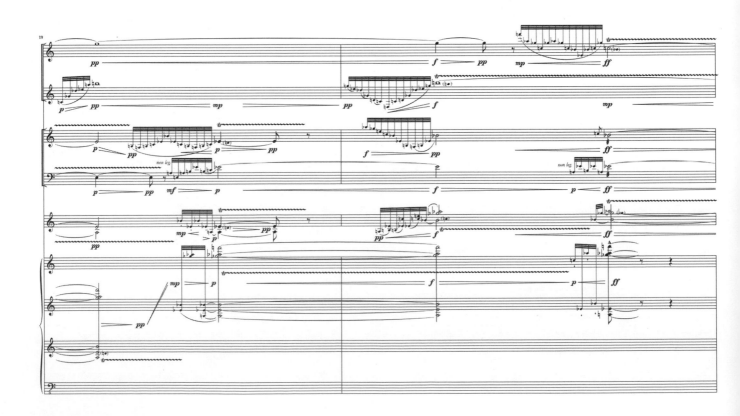

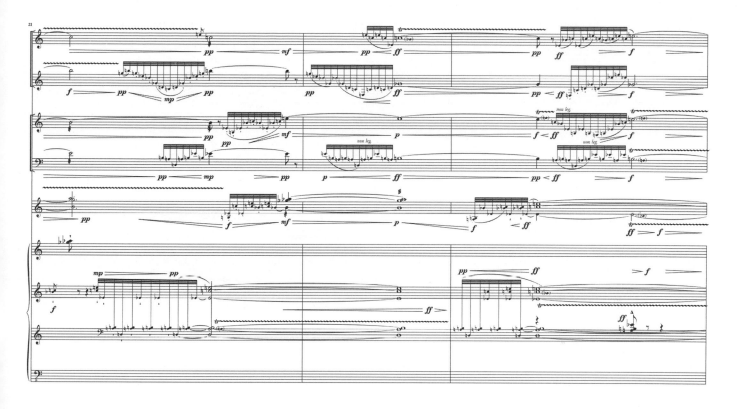

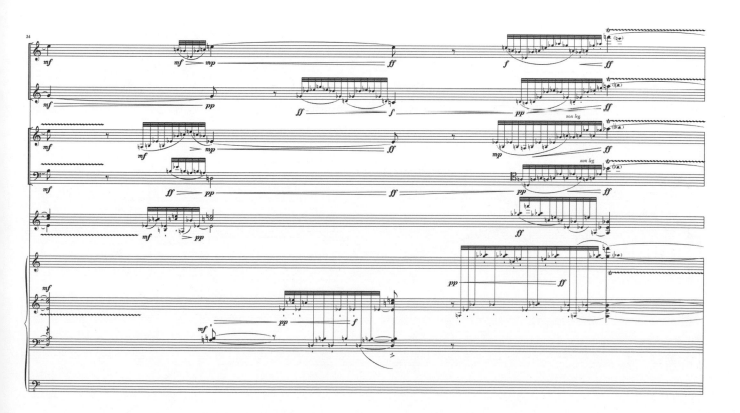

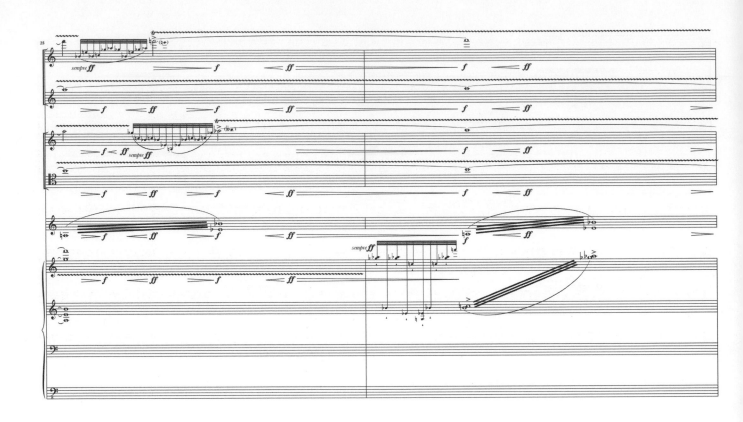

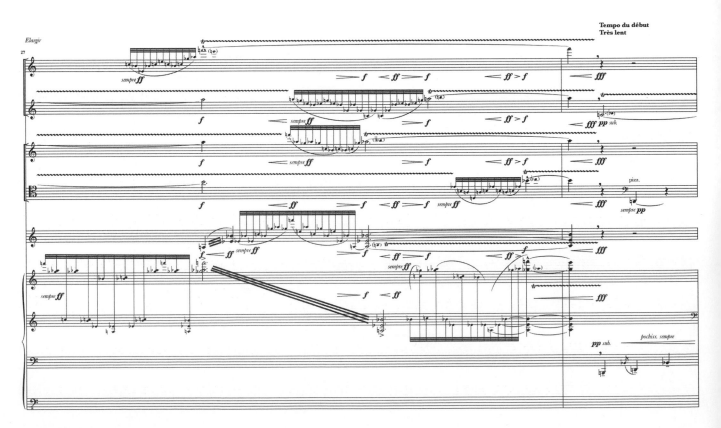

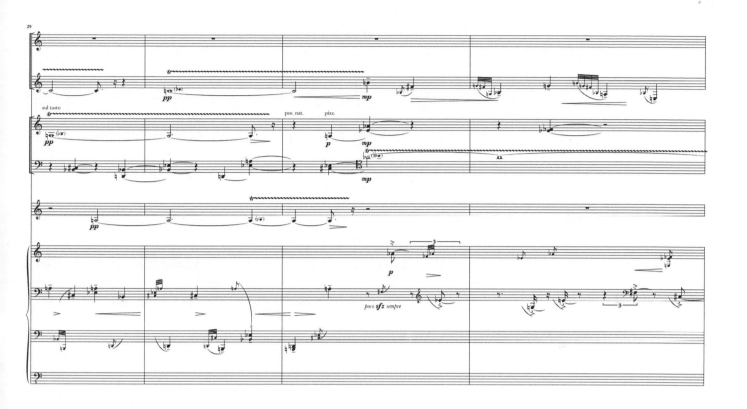

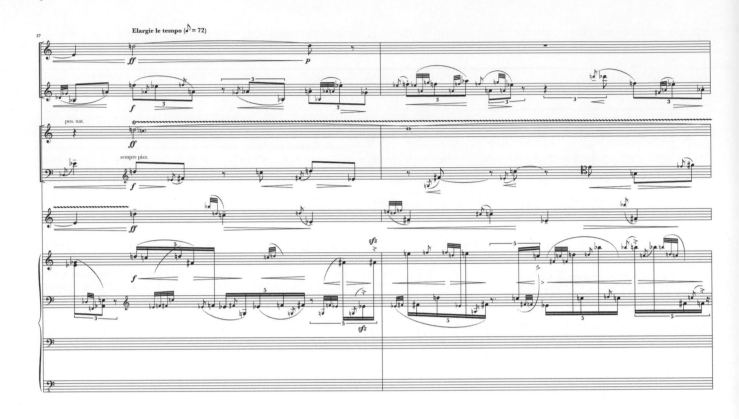

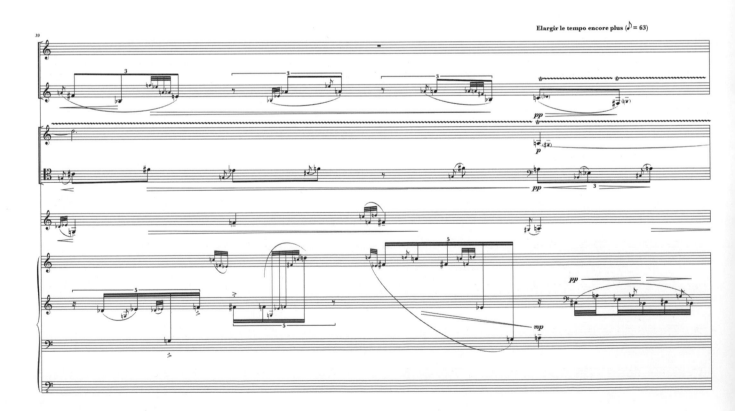

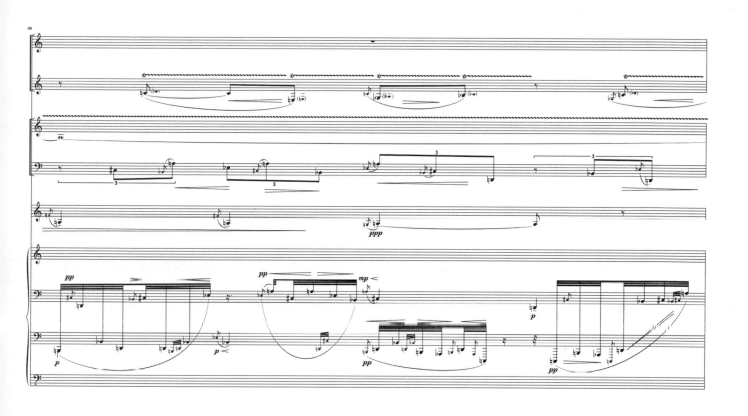

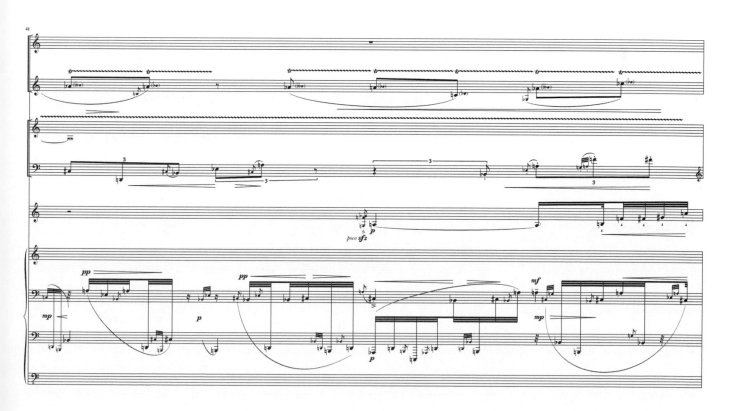

Elargir le tempo toujours davantage ($\flat$ = 60)

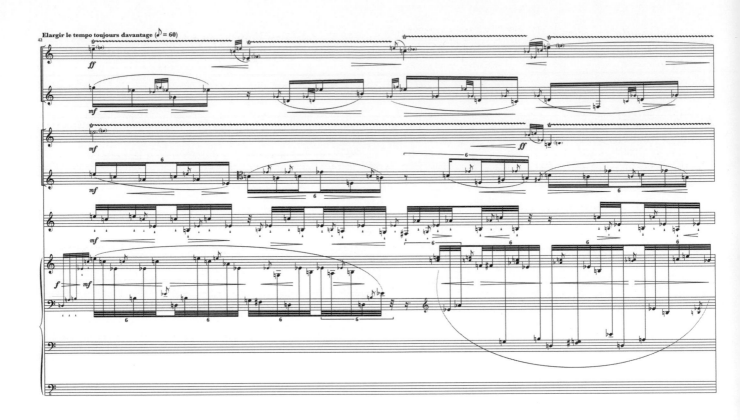

Reserrer le tempo vers le tempo initial ($\flat$ = 66)

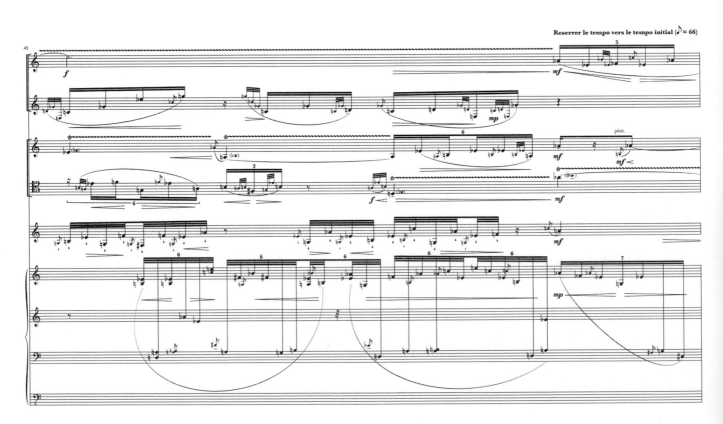

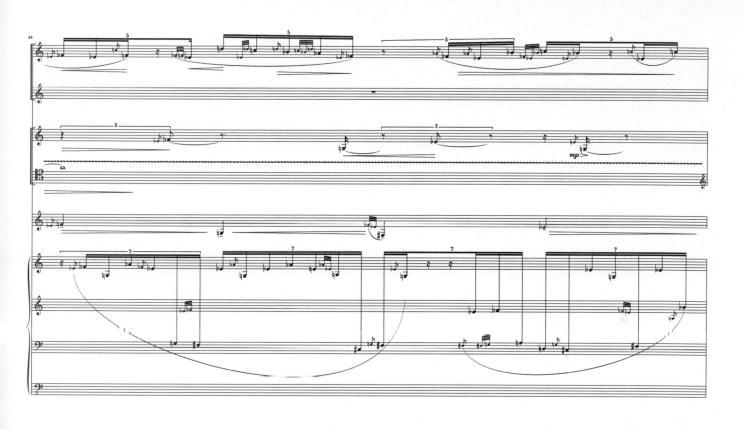

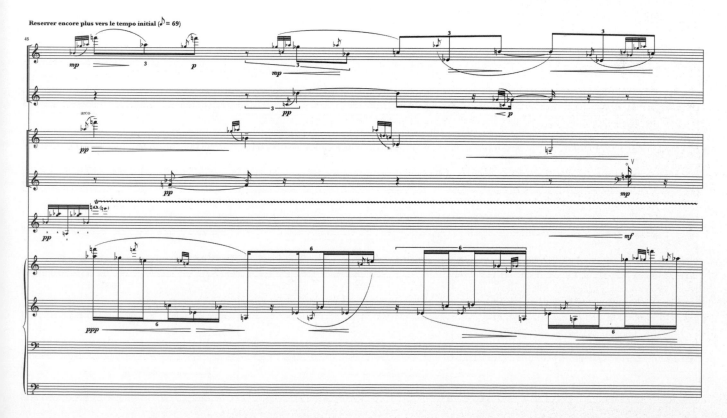

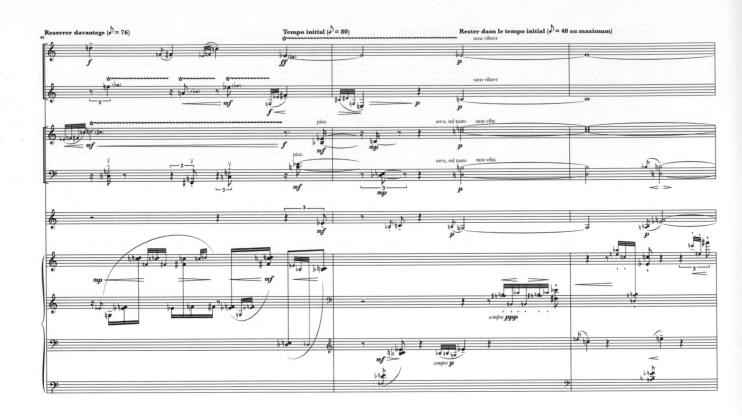

132. *Black Angels*
(1970)

GEORGE CRUMB
(1929–)
❖

George Crumb makes no secret of the influence that numerology had on his "electric" string quartet *Black Angels*. Can you hear instances of the numbers 7 and 13? Are these important for performers to elucidate? What of the use of the tritone ("the devil in music"), the [016] trichord, the *Dies Irae*, and the quotation of other pieces?

PERFORMANCE NOTES

1) All players read from score.
2) Each note is preceded by an accidental, except in case(s) of an immediate repetition of a pitch or a pattern of pitches. N.B.: the tonal passages are notated in the traditional manner.
3) The amplification of the instruments is of critical importance in BLACK ANGELS. Ideally, one should use genuine electric instruments (with a built-in pick-up). Otherwise, fine-quality contact microphones can be attached (by rubber bands) to the belly of the instrument. The player should find the best position for the microphone in order to avoid distortion of the tone. If the amplifier is equipped with a reverberation control, this should be set on "high" to create a more surrealistic effect. The dynamic level should also be extremely loud (for the forte passages) and the level should not be adjusted during the performance.
4) The following percussion instruments and special equipment will be needed:

a) Violin I: maraca
7 crystal glasses
solid glass rod (about 6 inches in length and 3/16 or 1/4 inch in diameter)
2 metal thimbles
metal plectrum (e.g. paper clip)

b) Violin II: tam-tam (suspended), about 15 inches in diameter
soft beater for the tam-tam
contrabass bow (for bowing tam-tam)
7 crystal glasses
solid glass rod (about 6 inches in length and 3/16 or 1/4 inch in diameter)
2 metal thimbles
metal plectrum (e.g. paper clip)

c) Viola: 6 crystal glasses
solid glass rod (about 6 inches in length and 3/16 or

metal plectrum (e.g. paper clip)

d) Cello: maraca
tam-tam (suspended) about 24 inches in diameter
soft beater for the tam-tam
very hard beater for the tam-tam (this should produce a percussive, metallic sound)
contrabass bow (for bowing tam-tam)

5) The crystal glasses (used for the "glass-harmonica" effect in God-music, on page 7) should be goblet-shaped (like wine glasses, with a stem). A fine grade of crystal will produce a truly beautiful effect. The glasses should be securely mounted on a board (by taping). The glasses can be

tuned by adding water, although the tone loses in purity if too much water is used. The following pitches are required (N.B.: the glasses sound one octave higher than written):

Violin I:

Violin II:

Viola:

6) The tam-tam harmonics are variable in pitch. The player should bow the "lip" of the tam-tam with a well-rosined contrabass bow.
7) All glissandi occupy the total duration of the note to which they are affixed. Use portamento only where indicated in the score.
8) All spoken sounds (whispering, shouting) must project! The whispered passages can be slightly voiced if the acoustics of the hall require this. The tongue clicks (in "Sounds of Bones and Flutes," on page 2) are percussive clicks off the upper palate (not clucking sounds).

9)   ♩ = a quarter tone higher than written pitch

   ♩ = a quarter tone lower than written pitch

   ▣ = fermata lunga

   ⌒ = normal fermata

   ′ = slight pause or "breath"

   ∕ = extremely short pause or "breath"

   tr(½) = trill a half step above principal note

   ·♩· = ♩♪   ·♩· = ♩♪

STAGE POSITIONING

(Sp.=Speaker, C.Gl.=Crystal Glasses, M.=Maraca)

PROGRAM

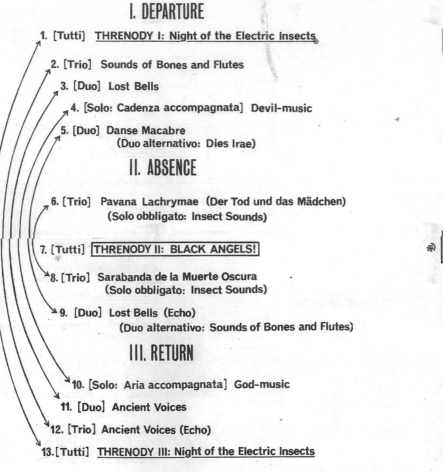

I. DEPARTURE

1. [Tutti]   THRENODY I: Night of the Electric Insects

2. [Trio]   Sounds of Bones and Flutes

3. [Duo]   Lost Bells

4. [Solo: Cadenza accompagnata]   Devil-music

5. [Duo]   Danse Macabre
        (Duo alternativo: Dies Irae)

II. ABSENCE

6. [Trio]   Pavana Lachrymae (Der Tod und das Mädchen)
        (Solo obbligato: Insect Sounds)

7. [Tutti]   THRENODY II: BLACK ANGELS!

8. [Trio]   Sarabanda de la Muerte Oscura
        (Solo obbligato: Insect Sounds)

9. [Duo]   Lost Bells (Echo)
        (Duo alternativo: Sounds of Bones and Flutes)

III. RETURN

10. [Solo: Aria accompagnata]   God-music

11. [Duo]   Ancient Voices

12. [Trio]   Ancient Voices (Echo)

13. [Tutti]   THRENODY III: Night of the Electric Insects

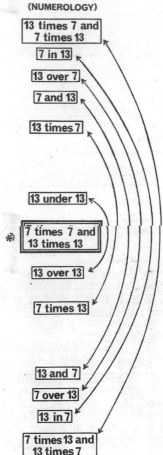

(NUMEROLOGY)

13 times 7 and
7 times 13

7 in 13

13 over 7

7 and 13

13 times 7

13 under 13

⁂ 7 times 7 and
13 times 13

13 over 13

7 times 13

13 and 7

7 over 13

13 in 7

7 times 13 and
13 times 7

⁂ This central motto is also the numerological basis of the entire work

Commissioned by the University of Michigan and Dedicated to the Stanley Quartet
(G. Ross, G. Rosseels, R. Courte, J. Jelinek)

[IMAGES I]

BLACK ANGELS

THIRTEEN IMAGES FROM THE DARK LAND
for Electric String Quartet

George Crumb
(in tempore belli, 1970)

I. DEPARTURE

1. Threnody I: Night of the Electric Insects [Tutti] 13 times 7 and 7 times 13

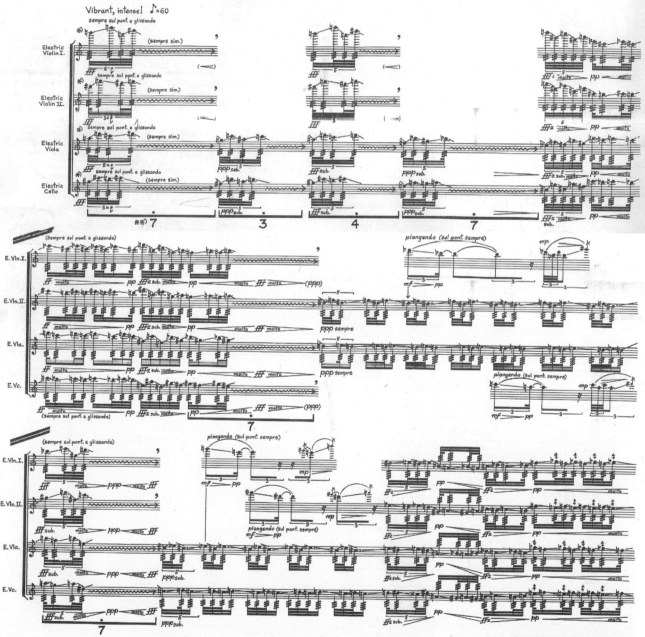

※) Make a continuous glissando, without dwelling on given pitches. The tremolo should be extremely rapid.

※※) The numbers under brackets indicate duration in seconds; and since quintuplet = 1 second, play 7 quintuplet groups in first bracket, 3 groups in second bracket, etc.

Edition Peters 66304

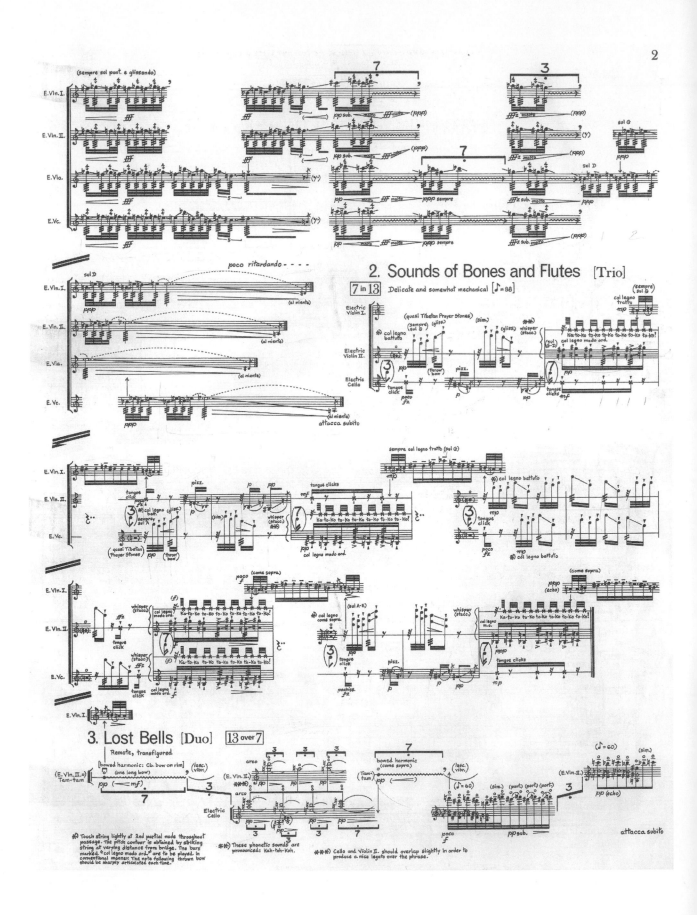

2. Sounds of Bones and Flutes [Trio]

Delicate and somewhat mechanical [♪=88]

3. Lost Bells [Duo]

Remote, transfigured

※) Touch string lightly at 2nd partial node throughout passage. The pitch contour is obtained by striking string at varying distance from bridge. The bars marked "col legno modo ord." are to be played in conventional manner. The note following thrown bow should be sharply articulated each time.

※※) These phonetic sounds are pronounced: Kah-toh-Koh.

※※※) Cello and Violin II. should overlap slightly in order to produce a nice legato over the phrase.

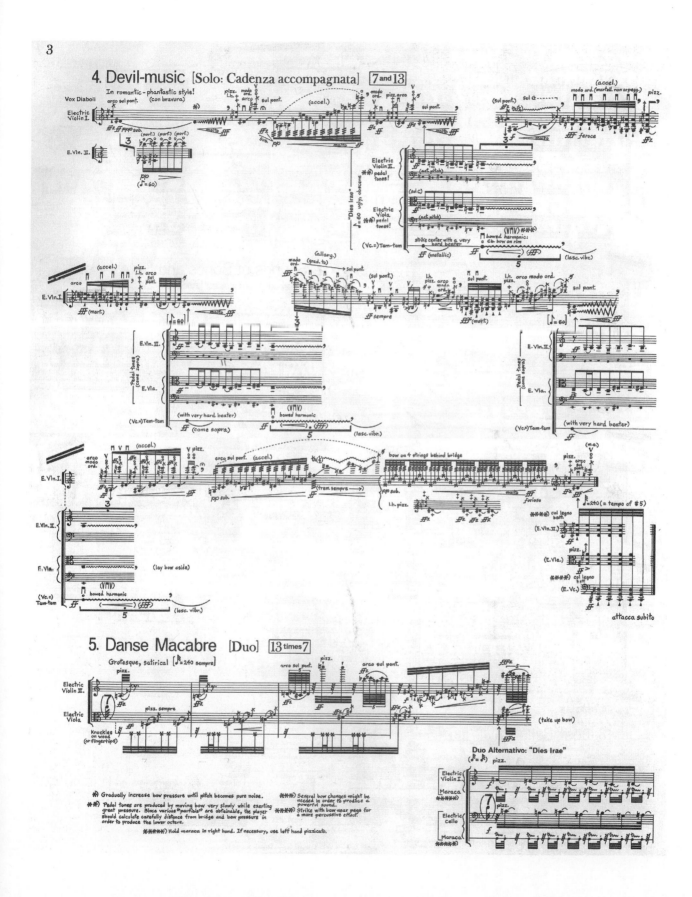

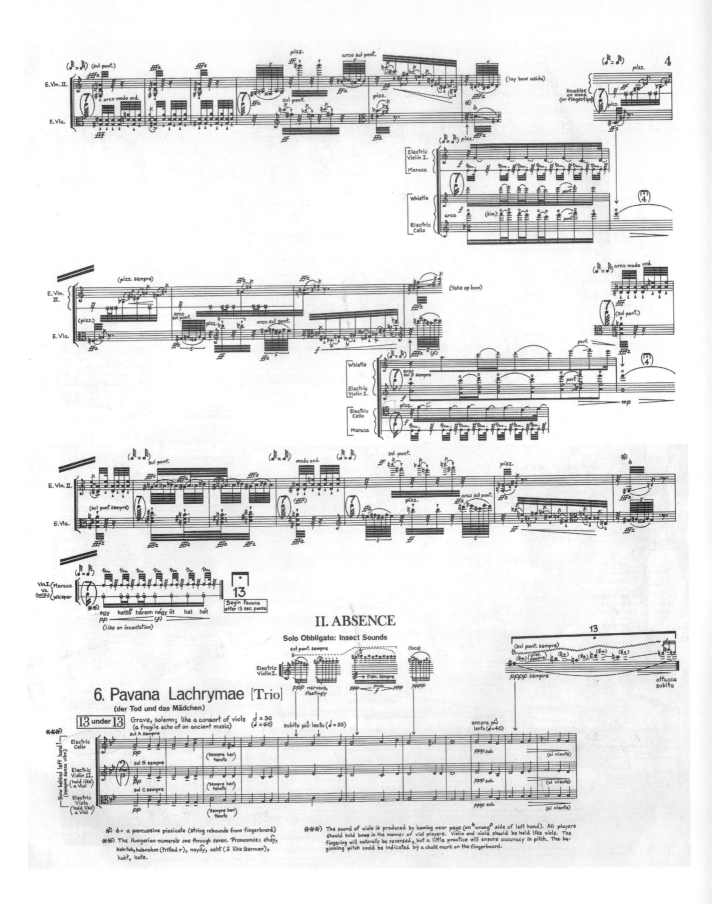

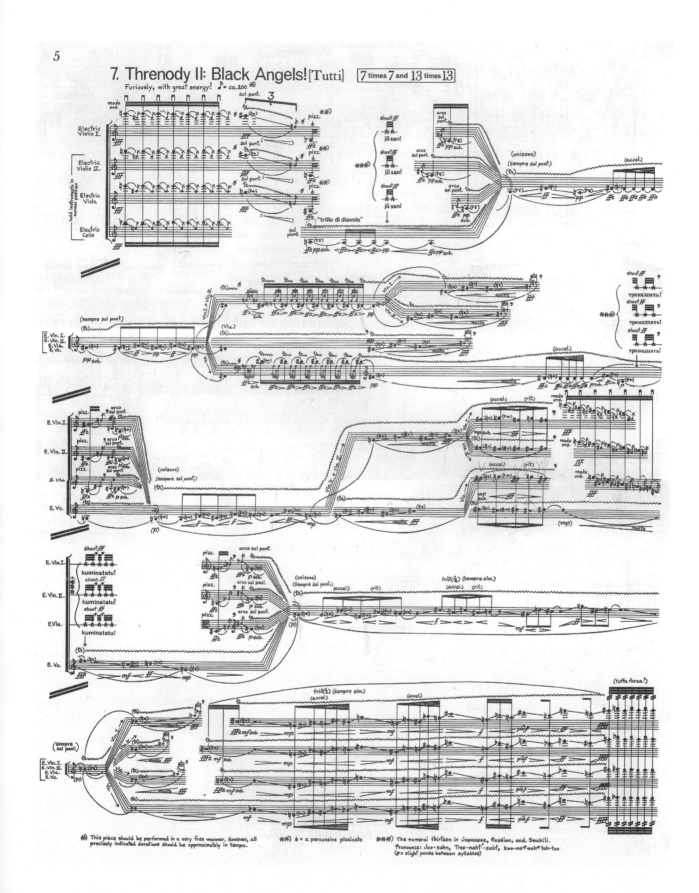

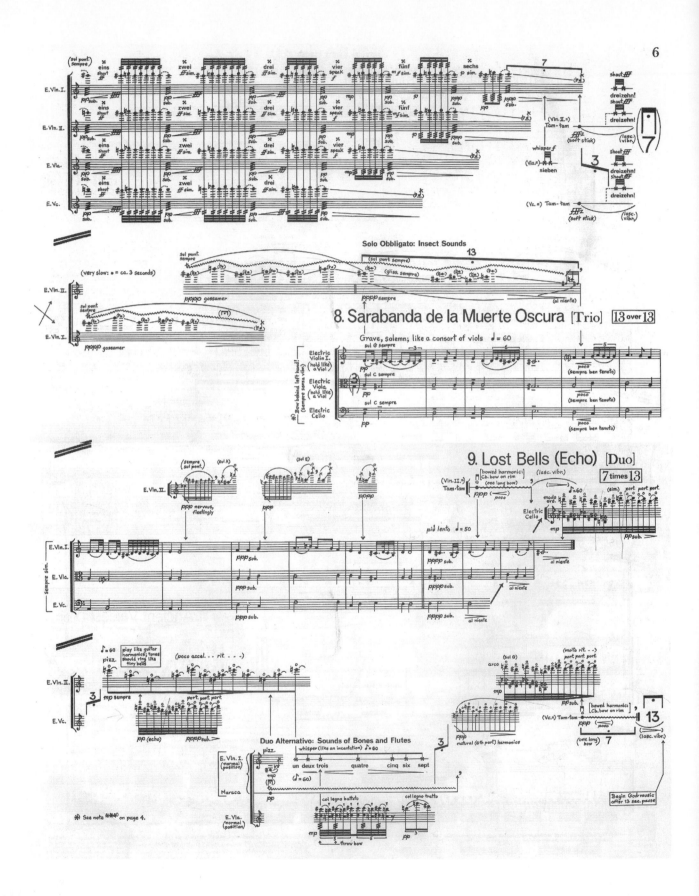

8. Sarabanda de la Muerte Oscura [Trio]

9. Lost Bells (Echo) [Duo]

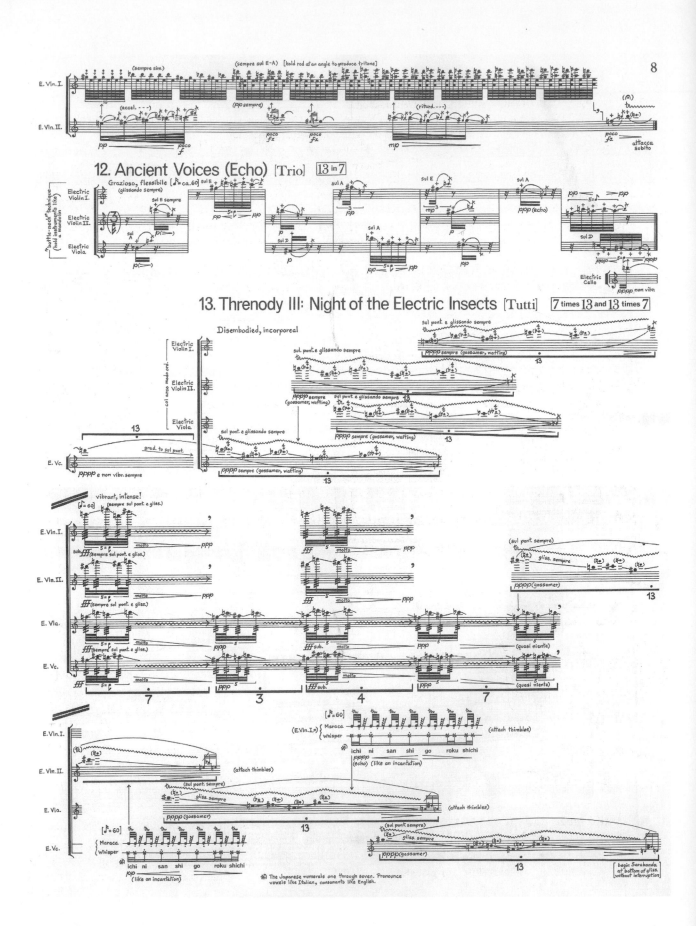

12. Ancient Voices (Echo) [Trio]

13. Threnody III: Night of the Electric Insects [Tutti]

Disembodied, incorporeal

9

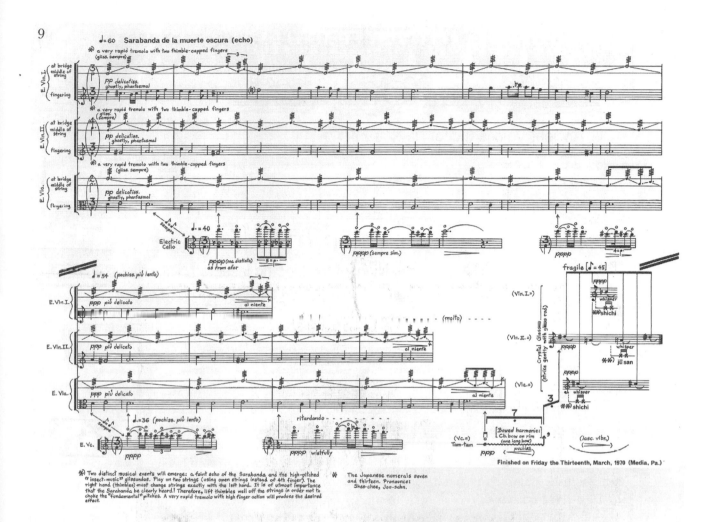

Sarabanda de la muerte oscura (echo)

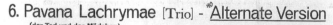

※ Two distinct musical events will emerge: a faint echo of the Sarabanda and the high-pitched "insect-music" glissandos. Play on two strings (using open strings instead of 4th finger). The right hand (thimbles) must change strings exactly with the left hand. It is of utmost importance that the Sarabanda be clearly heard! Therefore, lift thimbles well off the strings in order not to choke the "fundamental" pitches. A very rapid tremolo with high finger action will produce the desired effect.

※ The Japanese numerals seven and thirteen. Pronounce: Shee-chee, Joo-sahn.

Finished on Friday the Thirteenth, March, 1970 (Media, Pa.)

[APPENDIX]

6. Pavana Lachrymae [Trio] - <u>Alternate Version</u>
(der Tod und das Mädchen)

Grave, solemn; like a consort of viols

※ This version of the Pavana Lachrymae is overlaid with the Solo Obbligato: Insect Sounds (Violin I.), as in the original version (on page 4). The Solo Obbligato will cue into this version at precisely the same points. N.B. In this version the instruments are played in the normal manner, using sul tasto and senza vibrato to simulate the sounds of viols.

※※ Each successive note (of the series of notes under the arrow) should be slightly lower in pitch (in relation to the printed note) than the preceding note. The pitch falls almost imperceptibly until the last note of the series is precisely a half-tone lower than the printed pitch. In the cello part, for example, the first bar is played at true pitch; the first note of bar 2 is very slightly under a true G, the second note still slightly further under a true A, etc. This process continues until the last note of bar 3 actually sounds as E♯. Bar 4 is again notated at true pitch and in bar 5 the gradual flattening begins anew. The player thus "modulates" from g minor to f♯ minor to f minor. N.B. The three players must flatten pitches precisely together so that the intonation of any given chord is impeccable!

133. Andante from String Quartet No. 3 (1983)

ALFRED SCHNITTKE
(1934–98)
❖

Schnittke's musical style was multifaceted. Much of his music is disjointed and incongruous and often relies on quotation and illusion. Moreover, he had wide-ranging musical interests and affinities, from traditional genres such as the string quartet to more experimental electronic music. Some in Russia leveled anti-Semitic criticisms at Schnittke (who was born to a Jewish-Russian father and a German-Russian mother), calling him a "rootless cosmopolitan" because of his stylistic promiscuity and his contacts with the international music scene.

The third quartet is typical of Schnittke's "cosmopolitan" idiom, a collection of musical citations that epitomize his so-called polystylistic period. Listen for how the opening Renaissance cadence, with its stereotypical 4-3 suspension, is first unmade and then remade in the context of a twentieth-century post-tonal idiom. Musical materials based on the intervals of the minor second, perfect fourth, tritone, and perfect fifth combine with the Renaissance cadence and are presented with a number of idiomatic string techniques, among them glissando (sliding from one pitch to another), pizzicato (plucked, rather than bowed string playing), and *sul ponticello* (playing near the bridge, which creates a thin, attenuated timbre).

134. *Music for Pieces of Wood (1973)*

STEVE REICH

(1936–)

❖

In the second half of the twentieth century, a number of composers reacted to certain trends in modernist music. They felt music was often overly controlled, atomized, and oversaturated with detail and information. Rather than writing music whose complexity was not graspable by most audience members and that actively turned audiences away from contemporary music, composers such as Steve Reich wanted to find new organizational principles that would perhaps be accessible to a wider segment of the population.

Many of these composers wrote music that came to be known as "minimalist." "Minimalism" may be a bit of a misnomer; many of these works have their own sense of complexity and richness, and a number are long and involved. But the name stuck, in part because one of the obvious features of this music is the repetition of small segments of musical material with little or no change to them. (Note in this score there are changing dynamics that affect the entire set of repetitions. Thus, a crescendo written over a passage to be repeated between eight and twelve times would occur gradually across all the repetitions.) Variations enter the repetitions gradually and the listener often has a sense of witnessing an act of musical evolution in slow motion.

Reich is well known for a special kind of minimalist music known as phase music. Works such as *Violin Phase*, *Piano Phase*, and *Clapping Music* are all based on the phase principle, in which two iterations of the same musical material are played in unison followed by one of them being shifted slightly in time so it is "out of phase" with the other. The shifting continues, with the time gulf between the two segments of music widening until it begins to narrow again and the two segments eventually return to being "in phase" with one another. Along the way, the rhythmic interplay of the parts changes with each phase shift, bringing to the music both continuity and variety. Does an understanding of phase technique assist the analysis of *Music for Pieces of Wood*? If so, how? If not, what analytic concept or concepts seem more germane?

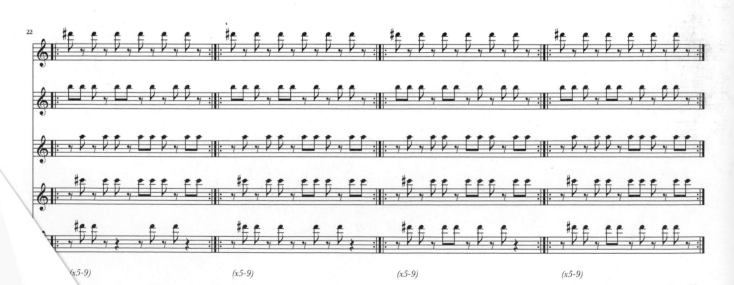

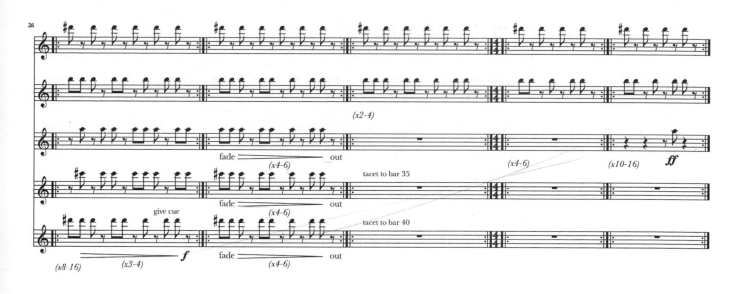

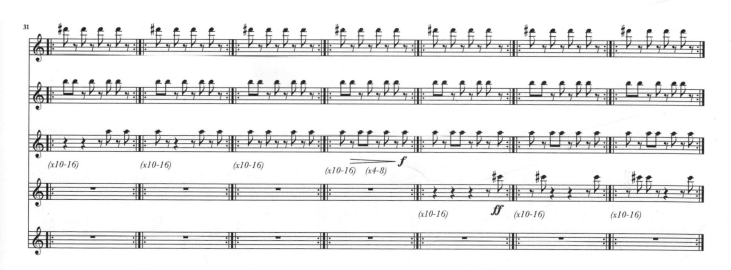

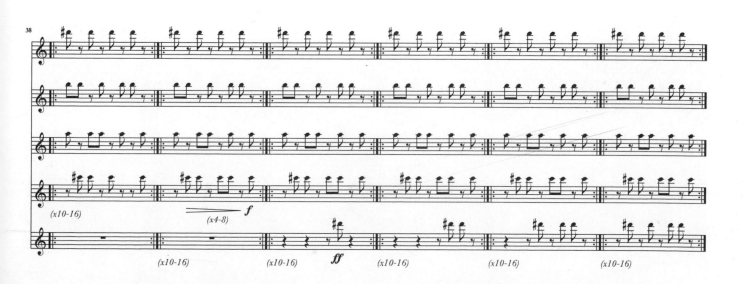

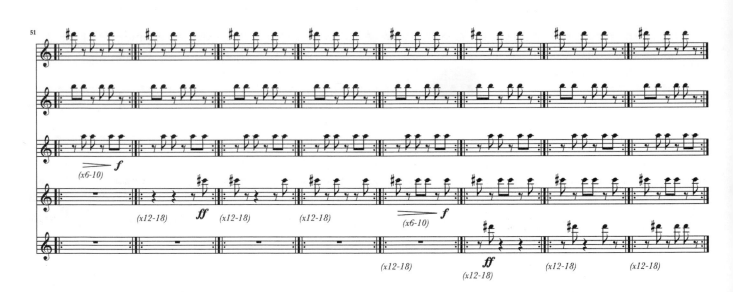

135. Excerpt from *Wings* *(1981)*

JOAN TOWER
(1938–)

❖

Joan Tower's early compositional practice drew heavily on serialism. As she matured as a musician, Tower found inspiration in the music of Olivier Messiaen and George Crumb. Do you hear *Wings,* for solo clarinet, illustrating any of these influences?

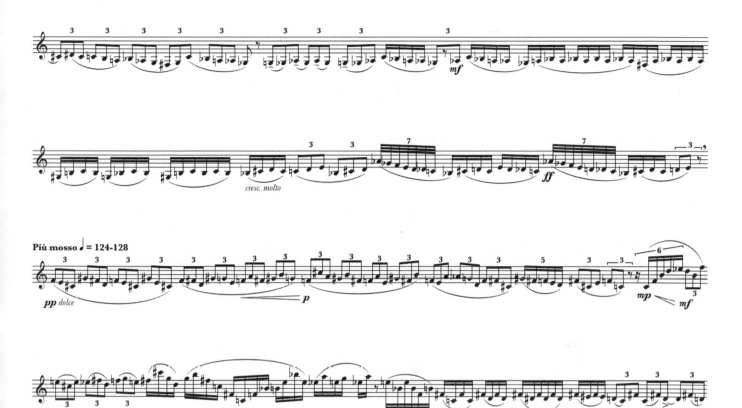

136. *Charm*
(2008)

JAMES DILLON
(1950–)

❖

Although many of James Dillon's scores do contain the hallmarks of "New Complexity", his use of these compositional techniques derives more from an eclectic and universalist approach to the materials of music than from a certain compositional system. Dillon's musical voice has been shaped in large part by his experience with and study of Scottish pipe-band music, rock music, North Indian music, jazz, Delta blues, and European art music. Among the latter, the music of Varèse and Xenakis has proved especially important to Dillon, whose preference for organizing evolving sound masses rather than structuralism echoes the orientation of these earlier composers.

Dillon's short piano piece *Charm* certainly doesn't fit the description of "New Complexity." Rather, its clear textures engage with the sonic world of turn-of-the-century French music, featuring whole-tone harmonies and a streaming of musical ideas separated by register (low pedal tones, high sound masses, and the main center of melodic movement in the middle register) and with short nineteenth-century piano works such as Beethoven's bagatelles, Op. 119. As with many of Dillon's works, the opening gesture is of paramount significance: a brief lick provides a preview of what will become a more languorous thematic statement throughout much of the work. Cast in a loose ternary (ABA) form, the return of the opening material at the end of the work is informed by what happens in the contrasting middle section. This is not to say that there aren't processes at work within each section. How, for instance, do the rhythmic subdivisions change over time in the opening A section?

Piano

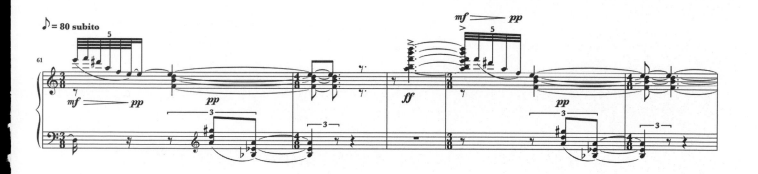

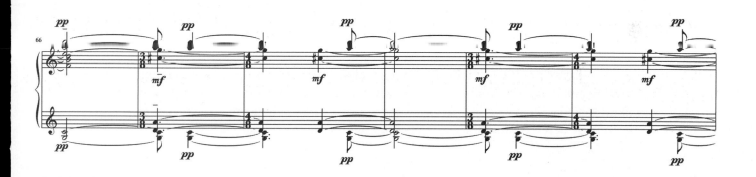

Appendix:

Sample Analysis and Performance Lesson Plan

THE FOLLOWING IS a possible 50-minute analysis-and-performance lesson plan on Robert Schumann's song, "Widmung," to be worked into the second half of a class devoted to chromatic modulation (most likely in the second year of a standard harmony sequence). It presumes knowledge of modal mixture, the Neapolitan, and some previous familiarity with the German Romantic lied.

Class Content and Outline of Activities

ACTIVITY	TIMING
A. Performance I	5 min.
B. Textual and Formal Analysis	5 min.
C. Motivic Analysis	20 min.
D. Harmonic and Tonal Analysis	15 min.
E. Performance II	5 min.

A. Begin by asking for a complete performance by the singer and pianist who volunteered to prepare and perform the piece. Ask the class to follow along with the score and note anything of musical or analytic interest.

B. After the performance, begin with an examination of the text. Throughout this discussion, involve both the class and the performers. What form does the poem take? Has the composer altered the poem at all in setting it to music? Why might he have done so? Discuss also the meaning of the text and its deeply dualistic portrayal of love. The beloved provides both joy and pain and is both death and salvation. Moreover, the beloved is both other and a component of self. What is the form of the music (ternary), and how does it relate to the form and/or meaning of the text?

C. Ask the performers if there were any recurring motives they sought to bring out. One worthy of mention is the suspension, "sigh," figure that first appears in m. 7 on the word "lebe." The accented dissonance resolving down by step is used to highlight other important words in the text. What are these? (*schwebe, wert, verklärt,* and arguably *liebend über mich*) How could they be performed to best effect? (like all accented dissonances, by leaning on the downbeat) Ask the performers to try a couple of these. Next, examine how the modulation into and out of E Major is achieved. From m. 13 to m. 14, the modulation is abrupt, making use of the G♯/Ab common tone between the two keys. Are these keys closely related? Why might Schumann have chosen a foreign-key relationship for this modulation? How might this be most effectively performed? Ask the performers to try it. What about the modulation back to Ab? This one is more interesting. Note that the IV chord in E major functions as a chromatic pivot chord, being the enharmonic Neapolitan in Ab Major. There is a motivic connection across this enharmonic seam as well. Not only does the sigh/suspension motive appear on the word *verklärt* over IV of E Major, but the resultant C♯ is itself transformed into an accented, dissonant Db over the V^7 of *liebend,* resolving down by half-step to C on *mich.* These two measures probably demand the most subtlety and sensitivity in performance of any in the song. Brainstorm ideas for how to perform them, and try two or three ways. What seems to work best? Why?

D. Begin by asking the performers and the class where the first instance of chromaticism occurs (the Fb in m. 5 on "Schmerz"). Is this significant? (Yes! It is both an example of mixture-as-word-painting, and a surface-level foreshadowing of the E-major B section.) Note that Schumann has made this note longer than the other arpeggiated notes in the piano accompaniment. A slight accent and/or tenuto mark in the piano part could also be appropriate. Ask the performers to try this a couple times. Look, then, for other examples of chromaticism. Within their local key context, are these examples of mixture (borrowing), applied chords (secondary dominants), or something else? How do they relate to the text?

E. Finally, close with one more performance. Forewarn the performers that you will speak while they are performing so as to remind them and the class of the points made about the song as they occur in real time. Ask the performers and the class afterward if and how the quality of the performance changed from the first time to the last time.

ASSIGNMENT: Choose two recordings available in the school library, in your private collection, or through online resources. In a two-to-four-page paper, critically compare the two performances with regard to the components of "Widmung" discussed in class, to wit: formal distinction of the middle section through tone color, dynamics, rubato, or other means; projection of the suspension/sigh motive; how the chromatic modulations were handled; color changes for important mixture chords; and so forth. Did either performance direct you toward aspects of the piece that weren't discussed in class? Did either performance affect how you might analyze the song?

Glossary of Foreign Terms

A-Saite: On the A string

A tempo: Back to (the original) tempo

Aber: But

Abwogend: Rising and falling

Ad libitum: At (your) liberty

Adagio: Slowly

Agitato: Agitated(ly)

Affettuoso: Affectionate(ly)

Al niente: To nothing

Alla breve: In cut time

Allargando: Broad(ly)

Alle Menschen müssen sterben: All men must die

Allegretto: Somewhat quick(ly)

Allegro: Happy (happily), quick(ly), up-beat

Allmählig: Gradually

Als das erste mal: Like the first time

Amabilmente: Pleasant(ly)

Amoroso: Amorous(ly)

Ancora: Repeat

Andante: Relaxed, walking tempo

Andantino: More motion than andante

Animant: Animated(ly)

Animato: Animated(ly)

Animé: Animated(ly)

Appassionato: Passionate(ly)

Aperto: Open

Arco: Bowed

Articulato: Articulated

Assai: Very

Attaca: Continue to the next movement without pausing

Äußerst: Extremely

Ausdruckvoll: Full of expression

Avivando: Lively

Barocco: Baroque

Beaucoup: Much

Begleitend: Accompanied

Ben: Good, well

Bewegt(er): With motion

Bouché cuivré: Hand stopped

Bravura: Skill or cleverness

Breit: Broad

Brillante: Brilliantly

Brio: Bright(ly)

Brutale: Brutal(ly)

Calando: Flagging

Calma: Calm(ness)

Calmando: Calm down

Calmandosi: Calming down

Calmato: Calm down

Canone al rovescio: Inversion canon

Cantabile: In a singing style

Cantando: Singing

Capriccioso: With caprice

Cédez: Hold back

Col legno: With the wood (of the bow)

Colla: With

Come: Like, as if

Comme la trompe de chasse: Like a hunting horn

Con: With

Corto: Short

Da capo: Return to the beginning

Dämpfer: Mute

Dans tout ce passage, les durées des notes sont maximales dans le mesure du possible: Throughout the entire passage, the notes' durations are as long as possible

Davantage: More

Deciso: Decisive(ly)

Declamando: Declaiming, in a declamatory manner

De très loin: From far off

Di nuovo: New

Die tiefere Oktav kann notfalls wegbleiben: The lower octave can be omitted if necessary

Doigté: Fingering

Dolce: Sweet, sweetly

Doloroso: Painful(ly), sorrowful(ly)

Doux: Sweet. sweetly

Durchlassen: Penetrating

Effekt: Effect

Eilen: Rush(ing)
Élargi: Grand, enlarged
Elegante: Elegant(ly)
Eleganza: Elegance
Empfindung: Sensitivity
Emporté: Taken away, let go
Encore plus: Again, more
En dehors: Outside
En retenant jusqu'à la fin: Held back up until the end
Encore: Again
Energetico: Energetically
Enfoncer et relever: Push in and lift up
Espansione: Expansion, expansiveness
Espressivo: Expressive(ly)
Etwas: Some or somewhat
Expressif: Expressive(ly)
Feierlich: Solemnly
Feuer: Fire
Flatterzunge: Fluttertongue
Flautando: In a flutelike manner
Flessibile: Flexible (flexibly)
Fließend: Flowing
Forza: Force
Fulgurant: Like a flash of lightning
Fuoco: Fire
Gebunden: Legato
Gedehnt: Stretched
Genau: Exact
Gesangvoll: Songful
Gestopft: Stopped
Gestrichen: Stroked
Geteilt: Divided
Getragen: Supported
Giusto: Correct, right, just
Grazioso: Gracefully
Grave: Extremely slow, dirgelike
Griffbrett: On the fingerboard
G-Saite: On the G string
Gut: Good, well
Harmonieux: Harmonious(ly)
Hervortretend: Emerging
Höhepunkt: Climax
Immer: Always, throughout
Immuable: Unchanging
Impalpable: Impalpable/impalpably
Impetuoso: Impetuous(ly)
Incisif: Incisive

Intènse: Intense(ly)
Intenso: Intense(ly)
Innigster: Intimately
Joyeaux: Joyous(ly)
Jusqu'à la fin: Up until the end
Kurz: Short
L'aise: Ease
Ländlermelodie: A German folk-dance melody
Laissez vibrer: Let (it) vibrate
Langsam: Slow(ly)
Larghetto: Somewhat slow
Largo: Very slow(ly)
Lebhaft: Lively
Legato: Smooth, connected
Légèrement: Light(ly)
Leggiero: Light(ly)
Leggiermente: Light(ly)
Leicht: Light(ly)
Lent: Slow(ly)
Lentement: Slowly
Lento: Slow(ly)
Librement: Freely
L'istesso tempo: The same tempo
Loco: In the same octave as written
Lointain: Far-removed
Lunga: Long
Ma: But
Maestoso: Majestic(ally)
Mais: But
Mais voici que Pan de sa flute recommence à jouer: But here Pan begins playing his flute once again
Marcato: Marked (articulation)
Marcia: March
Marqué: Marked (articulation)
Marsch funèbre: Funeral march
Martellato: Hammered
Mäßig: Moderate(ly)
Meno: Less
Mesto: Mournful, melancholy
Mezza/mezzo: Half
Misterioso: Mysteriously
Mit: With
Moderato: Moderate(ly)
Modéré: Moderate(ly)
Molto: Very, or much
Morendo: Dying away
Mormoramente: Murmuring, in a murmuring manner

Mosso: Motion (speed)

Moto: Motion

Mouvement: Movement

Muerte: Dead

Nervoso: Nervous(ly)

Nicht: Not

Non: Not

Ohne: Without

Ordinaire: Ordinary

Oscura/o: Dark

Otez: Remove

Ouvert naturel: Open, natural

Passionato: Passionately

Patetico: Pathetic(ally)

Perdendosi: Losing energy

Pesante: Heavy

Petites notes: sans hâte: Grace notes not rushed

Peu: Little, a little

Peu à peu: Little by little

Piacere: At your pleasure, ad libitum

Più: More

Pizzicato: Plucked

Plus: More

Poco: A little

Poco a poco: Little by little

Precipitoso: Hasty, hastily

Preciso: Precisely

Presser: Move forward

Pressez ce trait: Move the line forward

Presto: Very fast

Prestissimo: Extremely fast

Proclamato: Proclaimed, in a proclamatory manner

Qu'au debut: Like the beginning

Quasi: Somewhat, something of a

Questo: This

Questo pezzo si deve trattare colla più gran delicatezza: This piece must be handled with the most extreme delicateness

Ralentir: Slowing down

Rallantando: Slowing down

Rapide: Rapid(ly)

Rasch: Quick(ly)

Religioso: Religious(ly)

Reprenez: Resume

Resserrer: Narrow, or tighten

Resta concentrata: Remain concentrated

Rester dans: Rest in/at

Retenu: Kept, retained

Ripiglio: Recover, regain

Risoluto: Resolute(ly)

Robuste: Robust

Ruhig: Calm(ly)

Ruvido: Coarse, rough

Rythmé: Rhythmically

Sanft: Gentle/gently

Sans: Without

Schalltrichter auf: Bell up

Schleppen: Dragged

Schmeichelnd: Flatteringly

Schnell: Quickly

Schwacher werden: Becoming weaker

Scuotendosi: Shaking, shaken

Sec: Dry

Sehr: Very, or much

Semplice: Simple, simply

Sempre: Always, or throughout

Sereno: Serene(ly)

Seul(e): Alone

Sfrenato: Wild

Silenzio assoluto: Absolute silence

Simile: In the same manner

Solo: Alone

Sopra: On, onto, upon

Sordino: Mute

Sostenuto: Sustained

Sotto: Partial, partially

Soutenu: Sustained

Staccato: Detached, short

Stringendo: Tightening/accelerating

Subitement, presque le double plus lent sans trainer: Immediately, twice as slowly, but without dragging

Subito: Immediately

Sul ponticello: On the bridge

Sul tasto: On the fingerboard

Supplichevole: Imploring

Surtout: Throughout

Suspendu: Suspended

Tais-toi, contiens ta joie, écoute: Be quiet, contain your enthusiasm, listen

Takt: Beat

Tempo de début: Tempo of the beginning

Tempo initial: Beginning tempo

Teneramente: Tenderly

Tenuto: Hold, sustain

Tranquillo: Tranquil(ly)

Tratto: Stroke

Trauermarsch: Funeral march

Tre cordi: Three strings (release the una corda pedal)

Très: Very

Tristezza: Sadness

Troppo: Too much

Tutti: All together

Una corda: One string (depress the una corda pedal)

Un(e): A

Unabhängig vom a tempo kadensieren: Independent of the cadential tempo

Und: And

Vers: Around, about

Viel Bogen Wechseln: Many bow changes

Vif: Lively

Vigoroso: Vigorously

Vite: Quickly

Vivace: Lively

Voce: Voice

Wehmütig: Wistful(ly)

Wie am Anfang: Like at the beginning

Wie aus der Ferne: As if from a distance

Wie ein Hauch: Like a breath

Zart: Sweetly

Zurückhältend: Pulling back

Credits

The author would like to thank the following rights holders for permission to reprint the scores listed below.

Works Cited

Beach, David. 1998. "An Analysis of Schubert's 'Die Neugierige': A Tribute to Greta Kraus." *Canadian University Music Review* 19/1: 69–80.

———. 1987. "The First Movement of Mozart's Piano Sonata in A Minor, K. 310: Some Thoughts on Structure and Performance." *Journal of Musicological Research* 7: 157–79.

Berry, Wallace. 1989. *Musical Structure and Performance*. New Haven: Yale University Press.

Bribitzer-Stull, Matthew. 2003. "Contention in the Classroom: Encouraging Debate and Alternate Readings in the Undergraduate Theory Class." *Journal of Music Theory Pedagogy* 17: 21–45.

Brumbeloe. 2000. "Patterns and Performance Choices in Selected Perpetual-Motion Movements by J. S. Bach." *Theory and Practice* 25: 1–25.

Burkhart, Charles. 1994. "Mini-bar Downbeat in Bach's Keyboard Music." *Journal of Music Theory Pedagogy* 8: 3–26.

Cone, Edward. 1968. *Musical Form and Musical Performance*. New York: Norton.

Darcy, Warren. 2001. "Rotational Form, Teleological Genesis, and Fantasy-Projection in the Slow Movement of Mahler's Sixth Symphony." *19th-Century Music* 25/1: 49–74.

Excerpts cited from throughout the Minnesota High School Music Listening Contest Study Guides, written by Matthew Bribitzer-Stull © 2009–2011 editions.

Folio, Cynthia. 1991. "Analysis and Performance of the Flute Sonatas of J. S. Bach: A Sample Lesson Plan." *Journal of Music Theory Pedagogy* 5.2: 133–59.

Gauldin, Robert. 1991. "Beethoven's Interrupted Tetrachord and the Seventh Symphony." *Intégral* 5: 77–100.

Gjerdingen, Robert. 2007. *Music in the Galant Style*. New York: Oxford University Press.

Hatten, Robert. 1993. "Schubert the Progressive: The Role of Resonance and Gesture in the Piano Sonata in A, D. 959." *Intégral* 7: 38–81.

Krebs, Harald. 2004. "Hypermeter and Hypermetric Irregularity in the Songs of Josephine Lang." In *Engaging Music: Essays in Music Analysis*, ed. Deborah Stein. New York: Oxford University Press, 13–29.

Larson, Steve. 1983. "On Analysis and Performance: The Contribution of Durational Reduction to the Performance of J. S. Bach's Two-Part Inventions." *In Theory Only* 7.1: 31–45.

Leech-Wilkinson, Daniel. 2012. "Compositions, Scores, Performances, Meanings." *Music Theory Online* 18.1.4.

Lester, Joel. 1999. *Bach's Works for Solo Violin: Style, Structure, Performance.* Oxford: Oxford University Press.

Lewin, David. 1993. "A Transformational Basis for Form and Prolongation in Debussy's 'Feux d'artifice'." In *Musical Form and Musical Transformation: Four Analytic Essays.* New Haven: Yale University Press, 97–159.

Lowe, Bethany. 2003. "On the Relationship Between Analysis and Performance: The Mediatory Role of the Interpretation." *Indiana Theory Review* 24: 47–94.

Marvin, Elizabeth West. 1994. "Intrinsic Motivation: The Relation of Analysis to Performance in Undergraduate Music Theory Instruction." *Journal of Music Theory Pedagogy* 8: 47–57.

Marvin, Elizabeth West, and Marie Rolf. 1990. "Analytical Issues and Interpretive Decisions in Two Songs by Richard Strauss." *Intégral* 4: 67–103.

McClelland, Ryan. 2003. "Performance and Analysis Studies: An Overview and Bibliography." *Indiana Theory Review* 24: 95–106.

Nolan, Catherine. 1993. "Reflections on the Relationship of Analysis and Performance." *College Music Symposium* 33–34: 112–39.

Rink, John, ed. 1995. *The Practice of Performance: Studies in Musical Interpretation.* Cambridge: Cambridge University Press.

———. 2002. *Musical Performance: A Guide to Understanding.* Cambridge: Cambridge University Press.

Rothstein, William. 2005. "Like Falling off a Log: Rubato in Chopin's Prelude in A-flat Major Op. 28, No. 17." In *Performance and Analysis: Views from Theory, Musicology, and Performance*, ed. Timothy Koozin. Published by *Music Theory Online.*

Schachter, Carl. 1994. "Chopin's Prelude in D Major, Op. 28, No. 5: Analysis and Performance." *Journal of Music Theory Pedagogy* 8: 27–45.

Schmalfeldt, Janet. 2005. "Response to the 2004 SMT Special Session 'Performance and Analysis: Views from Theory, Musicology, and Performance'." In *Performance and Analysis: Views from Theory, Musicology, and Performance*, ed. Timothy Koozin. Published by *Music Theory Online.*

Stein, Deborah, ed. 2004. *Engaging Music: Essays in Music Analysis.* New York: Oxford University Press.

Stein, Deborah, and Robert Spillman. 1996. *Poetry into Song: Performance and Analysis of Lieder.* New York: Oxford University Press.

Vaughan, Victoria. 2002. "Music Analysis in the Practice Room." *British Journal of Music Education* 19.3: 255–68.

Wheelock, Gretchen. 1993. "Schwartze Gredel and the Engendered Minor Mode in Mozart's Operas." In *Musicology and Difference*, ed. Ruth Solie. Berkeley: University of California Press, 201–21.

Youens, Susan. 1997. *Schubert, Müller, and* Die schöne Müllerin. Cambridge: Cambridge University Press.

NOTE: The bibliographies in Folio (1991), 153–59; and McClelland (2003), 100–106, contain many additional references for those who wish to investigate the analysis-and-performance literature further. See also the issue of *Music Theory Online* (18.1) devoted to analysis and performance.

Index of Pieces
by Instrumentation

Flute (and piccolo)	24, 33, 37, 45, 56, 90, 94, 109, 111, 113, 116, 128, 131
Oboe (and English horn)	21, 35, 62, 64, 68, 73, 113, 116, 123, 126, 128
Clarinet (including Eb, A, and bass)	64, 73, 66, 79, 83, 109, 110, 116, 119, 128, 131, 135
Saxophones	32, 76, 113, 122, 125
Bassoon (and contrabassoon)	(17), (18), 19, 22, 47, 56, 109, 116, 126, 128
Trumpet	93, 109, 115
French horn	47, 52, 56, 74, 93, 116, 128
Trombone (tenor and bass)	(19), 69, 82, 84, 93, 109
Tuba	93, 99, 124
Marimba and other percussion	15, 27, 87, 131, 134
Guitar	57, 110, 113, 117, 121
Harp	33, 36, 113, 123
Piano	39, 41, 47, 48, 52, 53, 54, 55, 58, 59, 60, 61, (62), 63, 64, 65, 66, 67, 68, (69), 70, (72), 73, 74, 76, 77, 79, 80, 81, 82, 83, 84, 85, 88, 89, 903, 91, 95, 96, 97, 98, 101, 102, 103, 105, 106, 107, 115, 116, 119, 125, 127, 131, 136
Organ	20, 21, 33, 78
Harpsichord (or other keyboard)	17, 18, 19, 21, 22, 28, 29, 32, 34, 35, 37, 113
Violin	17, 18, 21, 30, 33, 34, 38, 44, 45, 46, 50, 53, 63, 108, 112, 118, 119, 120, 129, 131, 132, 133
Viola	21, 23, 33, 38, 45, 46, 50, 58, 67, 79, 108, 118, 120, 129, 132, 133
Cello	(17), (18), (19), 21, 31, 33, 38, 45, 46, 50, 52, 63, 77, 108, 118, 119, 120, 129, 131, 132, 133
Double bass	21, 33, 101, 106, 118, 130
Voice	1, 2, 3, 6, 7, 8, 9, 57, 60, 61, 62, 68, 72, 73, 91, 96, 97
Wind ensemble	42, 100, 122
Choral ensemble	10, 11, 13, 14, 16, 25, 41, 71, 75, 104
Full orchestra	40, 43, 49, 62, 69, 71, 72, 86, 92, 112, 114

NOTE: Numbers in parentheses denote pieces playable by the instrument in question, though the work in the anthology may not be listed as such.

Index of Compositional Materials and Techniques

The index below is not intended to be exhaustive—perish the thought of listing every major third or root-position triad!— but rather to provide some of the clearer or most significant examples of the listed compositional materials and techniques. Advanced, difficult, ambiguous, and debatable examples for the entries below do not appear unless noted specifically as such (e.g., instances of tonal ambiguity). Tracing hypermeasures in Bach's g-minor violin fugue or determining where the transition and second tonal area occur in Haydn's String Quartet Op. 72, No. 2, for example, could be wonderfully challenging exercises, but these aren't the sort of clear examples one might want to use in a class's first introduction to a topic. Many excerpts are cited under multiple headings. What one musician hears as tonicization, another may consider as a full-fledged modulation. Thus, inclusion in the index indicates only the possibility of labeling a given phenomenon in a certain way and not firm advocacy for doing so. Finally, note the formatting below; bold numbers indicate specific works listed in the Chronological List of Works by Composer followed by specific measure numbers if appropriate; references to measure zero (m. 0) indicate anacruses to the first complete measure.